C000174257

NETHERTON

NED WILLIAMS

SUTTON PUBLISHING

Sutton Publishing Limited
Phoenix Mill · Thrupp · Stroud
Gloucestershire · GL5 2BU

First published 2006

Reprinted 2006

Title page photograph: Netherton's Coronation
Carnival Queen, 1953: 14-year-old Jean
Homer of Lincoln Road. *(Harry Rose)*

British Library Cataloguing in Publication Data
A catalogue record for this book is available from the
British Library.

ISBN 0-7509-4182-0

Typeset in 10.5/13.5pt Photina.
Typesetting and origination by
Sutton Publishing Limited.
Printed and bound in England by
J.H. Haynes & Co. Ltd, Sparkford.

THE BLACK COUNTRY SOCIETY

The Black Country Society is proud to be associated with
Sutton Publishing of Stroud. In 1994 the society was
invited by Sutton Publishing to collaborate in what has
proved to be a highly successful publishing partnership,
namely the extension of the ***Britain in Old Photographs***
series into the Black Country. In this joint venture the Black
Country Society has played an important role in establishing and developing a
major contribution to the region's photographic archives by encouraging society
members to compile books of photographs of the area or town in which they live.

The first book in the Black Country series was *Wednesbury in Old Photographs* by
Ian Bott, launched by Lord Archer of Sandwell in November 1994. Since then
almost 70 Black Country titles have been published. The total number of
photographs contained in these books is in excess of 13,000, suggesting that the
whole collection is probably the largest regional photographic survey of its type in
any part of the country to date.

This voluntary society was founded in 1967 as a reaction to the trends of the
late 1950s and early '60s. This was a time when the reorganisation of local
government was seen as a threat to the identity of individual communities and
when, in the name of progress and modernisation, the industrial heritage of the
Black Country was in danger of being swept away.

The general aims of the society are to stimulate interest in the past, present and
future of the Black Country, and to secure at regional and national levels an
accurate understanding and portrayal of what constitutes the Black Country and,
wherever possible, to encourage and facilitate the preservation of the Black
Country's heritage.

The society, which now has over 2,500 members worldwide, organises a yearly
programme of activities. There are six venues in the Black Country where evening
meetings are held on a monthly basis from September to April. In the summer
months, there are fortnightly guided evening walks in the Black Country and its
green borderland, and there is also a full programme of excursions further afield by
car. Details of all these activities are to be found on the society's website,
www.blackcountrysociety.co.uk, and in *The Blackcountryman*, the quarterly
magazine that is distributed to all members.

PO Box 71 · Kingswinford · West Midlands DY6 9YN

CONTENTS

Dudley

The map shows the principal roads, canals and railways of Netherton, *c.* 1950. It also shows the boundaries very clearly, although the western boundary has been 'simplified' in order to accommodate the map on this page. The western boundary follows the Black Brook through Saltwells Wood but then seems to follow the centre of the Dudley No. 2 Canal up to Pear Tree Lane. The eastern boundary follows the course of the Mousesweet Brook although this is complicated by the fact that the river's course was much modified by the canal building in the Windmill End area, and then by the construction of the railway embankment carrying the Bumble Hole Line on its way between Dudley and Old Hill. The canal arm running parallel to St Peter's Road originally extended all the way to Baptist End – almost turning the centre of Netherton into an island. Note that the late lamented Cradley Heath Stadium, Mushroom Green and Saltwells Woods are all quite definitely in Netherton, although neighbours have tended to appropriate them. (Mushroom Green is not marked on this map but occupies the area just to the west of Quarry Road in the south-western corner of Netherton.) This is a composite map compiled from various sources. For a clear cartographic picture of Netherton as it was in the 1900s, readers are recommended to inspect the Alan Godfrey reprints of the old Ordnance Survey maps.

INTRODUCTION

A visitor to Netherton in the 1890s went looking for Netherton Hall. He took a path from Cinder Bank down into the shallow valley of the Black Brook. Eventually he came across the remains of the foundation walls and part of a doorway. To one side of this ruin was a large pit mound, on the other side another ruin which included premises that had once been the Old Bush, also known as the Black Boy. Nearby were some farm buildings, partly built with bricks salvaged from the hall. He learnt that the last occupier of the hall, Henry Guest, had left in the 1860s when his home began to collapse as a result of mining subsidence.

I think this story tells us that several Nethertons had come and gone by the end of the nineteenth century. Once upon a time there had been a Netherton which was just one of several hamlets south of Dudley, where there were manors and halls, scattered farms, and a thick bed of coal and other minerals waiting to be exploited. All this began to change dramatically at the end of the eighteenth century with the coming of turnpike roads and the canals.

The first half of the nineteenth century saw the landscape turned upside down by the exploitation of minerals, and industry began to take advantage of the new 'infrastructure' – particularly the canal. Small businesses turned into vast canal-side works and the population rapidly grew to provide a workforce. It was an unplanned and uncontrolled transformation, and it swiftly created a Black Country that had to be sorted out during the second half of the nineteenth century by the creation of new local government. Subsidence as the result of mining was a major problem, and the consequences of the population explosion were creating a new demand for planned streets, drainage, housing, education and health facilities.

Dudley was granted Borough status in 1865 and this was upgraded to County Borough in 1888. Its boundaries, as a 'detached' part of Worcestershire included Netherton and Woodside. Across the border in Staffordshire, Netherton's neighbours, Rowley Regis, Old Hill, Quarry Bank and Brierley Hill, were given Urban District status in the 1890s, but Netherton was already part of Dudley and enjoyed no such independence.

Dudley had many problems of its own to sort out in the second half of the nineteenth century, but Netherton's three representatives on the council made sure that progress in Dudley was quickly reflected in Netherton, often in parallel with Woodside. This could be in such matters as the provision of public libraries, or the massive reclamation of colliery wastelands and the laying out of new streets. Electric street lighting for example came to Netherton (and Woodside) on 24 November 1902.

It is interesting to note that in 1953 at the time of Elizabeth II's coronation several streets still had no mains electricity, let alone television sets.

The electric trams from Dudley to Old Hill and Cradley Heath via Netherton began running on 1 October 1900, only to be suspended four days later, and then 'officially opened' on the 19th! This event was to herald an Edwardian period of Netherton's expansion, when good quality housing and well-laid-out streets really began to transform the place. One only has to compare the picture of late Victorian Netherton on p. 19, where pit banks and subsidence are all too obvious, with the numerous postcard views of the town in its Edwardian heyday. (It is true that these postcard views tend to concentrate on central Netherton along its main highway and into roads like Church Road.)

My own acquaintance with Netherton began during my very first dramatic introduction to the Black Country in the autumn of 1962. I travelled from Old Hill to Dudley on the Midland Red 243 bus and my life was never the same again! Some time later I came into contact with the Cine Section of Dudley Photographic Society. We used to meet in a studio built above Little's shoe factory in Hill Street. I reached this by motorcycle – travelling across the Black Brook valley from Holly Hall – something of an adventure! Also, as a result of contact with the Photographic Society I met Nethertonians such as Bill Massey, who had taken an enormous number of photographs of Netherton in the 1960s.

One way to appreciate Netherton is to view it from the surrounding hills. Viewed from Rough Hill, above Springfield, in 2005, Netherton's hill-top church stands out clearly, as do the flats in Swan Street (right) and St John's Street (left). *(NW)*

Netherton was immediately an inspiration as a film location and one film made in about 1965, *The Morning Train*, made good use of Netherton's streets. Our fascination with these streets was partly their dereliction, and the process of demolition. Despite being aware of Bill Massey's photographs, and knowing that an old Netherton was being knocked down around us, I am ashamed to say that I still did not reach for my still camera and start recording Netherton's story from that time on.

Another of Netherton's personal attractions was the railway line traversing its eastern boundary – the Bumble Hole Line. I travelled on this on several occasions, including the last train on 13 June 1964, and even made a short film about it. The railway introduced me to Windmill End and it has always remained one of my favourite places, even although the railway's presence has been obliterated. There is a special magic about Windmill End's landscape: the canals, the tunnel, the pit banks and the long views. It also taught me that Netherton embraced a number of outlying communities: Windmill End itself, Darby End, Baptist End, the Saltwells, Mushroom Green, Lodge Farm, and so on. All these areas had undergone tremendous change before I knew them. They have also undergone further change in the period I have known them. The question I am left asking myself is: why didn't I start a 'Netherton Project' earlier?

Netherton from Windmill End. In the foreground is Cobb's Engine House, from which Henry Ford removed the engine in 1928! The canal, on its approach to the Netherton Tunnel, is hidden in its own cutting just behind the engine house. Beyond the new Sledmere Estate is Baptist End and the familiar Swan Street flats. Traversing the skyline leftwards we can pick out Hillcrest School, the chimney at Little's factory and the tower of Netherton's church. (*Keith Hodgkins*)

Did the Nethertonians explore Netherton? Well – some did! Jeff Parkes took his daughters Alison and Bonita on trips round Netherton from their home in Dudley Wood and took photographs as well! *Above left:* they climb the hill past Lodge Farm in 1961 with Round Oak Steel Works gracing the skyline, and only a track running across to the site we now know as the Merry Hill Centre. It is still good to walk from here into Saltwells Wood, or walk round the reservoir. *Right:* Alison and Bonita were left under no illusion that Netherton's story could be separated from the presence of coal. In the early 1960s a number of pit frames still stood in the Black Brook valley. *(Jeff Parkes)*

One of Harry Rose's early snaps shows a pit in the Saltwells area in the 1940s, with the Yew Tree Hills forming a hazy backdrop. *(Harry Rose)*

While asking myself why I hadn't made a better attempt to photograph Netherton or write about it, I could also ask myself what record others have made. It certainly wasn't that Netherton lacked interest. The Netherton Art Centre maintained a steady stream of productions that kept us coming to Netherton. These were provided by the likes of Dudley Little Theatre and Quarry Bank Amateur Operatic Society. The landscapes at Lodge Farm Reservoir, Saltwells Woods and Windmill End also attracted attention. Such places have frequently been visited by the Black Country Society's guided walks programme. Meanwhile, the Old Swan acquired a regional if not national reputation, as the production of home-brewed ale elsewhere faced extinction. The Black Country Museum was also drawn to Netherton: two Netherton buildings demanded re-creation at the museum – Emile Doo's shop and the Providence Chapel.

In Netherton itself it seems that people went to sleep as the town continued to change. However, there was an awakening in the early 1980s – a new sense of community and a desire to reinvigorate Netherton. The Netherton Community Association was formed in 1980 and Hillcrest School took on a community role. By 1985 there was the *Netherton News* with a circulation of 6,000. That spirit survives today in the Netherton Conservation Group, based at the Visitor Centre situated by the canal at Windmill End. Among the volunteers there are some interested in preserving Netherton's history and others who have modern environmental concerns. Elsewhere, there is the phenomenon of regeneration, in which local government and partners try to reinvent a sense of community, having identified that 'DY2' is in need of such attention.

The Midland Red 243 bus crawls through the centre of Netherton one Sunday in the early 1960s as the Scouts march behind their band. The Church of England School dominates the scene and the road sign on the corner of what was then Castle Street warns motorists to beware of schoolchildren. *(St Andrew's Collection)*

This book, then, appears at an interesting time. While compiling it I have watched the old Savoy cinema building in Northfield Road being demolished. This is a reminder that places that were once the 'old Netherton' vanish very easily. At the same time, the old fire station and police houses between the Savoy and the Art Centre are being restored and some attention has at last been paid to the park. Some features of 'old Netherton' have a future.

It seems a good time to collect old photographs and lay them out on these pages and share some memories with a generation of older Nethertonians who have had to watch the various dramatic changes. Let's remember nights at the Savoy, or even 'Bungies' in the days when the Art Centre building was the Public Hall or Institute. Let's remember just how industrial Netherton was, and before that how its landscape was so moulded by man's extraction of coal. Let's remember Emile Doo's shop when it was still in Halesowen Road – not in a museum – and in the wake of the closure of Noah's Ark, let's think back to all those hotbeds of nonconformity, now represented by 'Providence' in the Black Country Living Museum.

The Old Swan, 'Ma Pardoe's', is still in the centre of Netherton – and it's not just a museum piece – and there are still streets worth exploring, plus woods, canals, chapels and shops well worth visiting, and up on the hill Netherton's Victorian church still boldly battles with winds blowing up from the Bristol Channel, which you can probably see on a clear day. Come and enjoy Netherton!

The undefeated league champions: Darby End Wesley Bible Institute Junior Football Team of 1918/19. (*Betty Nash*)

1
Finding Your Way
Around Netherton

The centre of Netherton lies to the east of a hill surmounted by the parish church, encircled by the Dudley No. 2 Canal, and bisected by the old turnpike road from Dudley to Halesowen. It is the passage along this road that most people will understand, but many of the most fascinating parts of Netherton are at its extremities – well away from this road. Like all Black Country towns, Netherton yields surprises to those prepared to explore on foot.

The turnpike road (A459) leaves Dudley in the Blowers Green area and enters Netherton at Cinder Bank. To the east of the main road at this point is Baptist End, one of Netherton's satellite hamlets. The old Victorian heart of Netherton begins at the junction with Simms Lane, and from there to the town centre the road was once called High Street. High Street climbs at the approach to the centre and then bends as it becomes Halesowen Road. Victorian Netherton was built on both sides of this road from the town centre down to the Dudley No. 2 Canal at Bishton's Bridge, although Primrose Hill, to the west of the road, felt it was a community in its own right.

From Bishton's Bridge the Halesowen Road plunges towards Netherton's southern frontier: the Mousesweet Brook. The hamlets of Bowling Green, Darby End and Windmill End occupy the valley of the brook. In the remote south-west corner of Netherton, close to the confluence of the Mousesweet Brook and the Black Brook (once beneath the waters of the Cradley Pool) were the hamlets of Dudley Wood and Mushroom Green.

Cinder Bank, at the Simms Lane junction, being resurfaced in the 1920s. The Hope Tavern and the houses seen here still exist today. *(Dudley Archives)*

Swan Street in the mid-1960s, looking down towards the People's Mission. Park Road, on the right, was built in the 1900s when the park, or recreation ground, first opened. The shop, G.H. Hoskins, was typical of Netherton's little corner shops which sprang up with each new phase of house building. Swan Street leads down into Baptist End. *(Dudley Archives)*

This picture and the one opposite can be seen as one long panoramic view taken from High Street, looking down Baptist End Road on this page, and down Arch Hill Street on the opposite page, with Grainger's butcher's shop on the extreme left (currently a sandwich shop) and Holden's Garage at the road junction. These photographs date from 1963. *(Dudley Archives)*

Flags out in St Thomas Street for the coronation, looking towards St John's Street, 1953. St Thomas Street ran through the centre of the triangle created by High Street, St John's Street and Simms Lane – very much the result of the Victorian expansion of Netherton. Today it has been truncated and redeveloped almost out of existence but the Liberal Club is still there in a much-altered Victorian building. *(Harry Rose)*

Arch Hill Street was laid at the end of the 1890s as one approach to the new recreation ground, which became Netherton Park. The trees stand on the falling ground of the park, the fall of which continues down Baptist End Road into the upper valley of the Black Brook. *(Dudley Archives)*

Leaving the Turnpike Road axis and proceeding up Simms Lane, this is Hill Street and the 'remote' westernmost limits of Victorian Netherton. The land west of Hill Street was then empty unstable colliery waste – and it is still open space today. In 1981 a West Midlands Travel bus pauses in Hill Street, opposite the old Little's shoe factory. *(NW)*

In Edwardian times Blackbrook Road bravely pushed westwards and then gave up as the road, now closed to vehicles, descended into the Black Brook valley. The solidly built houses look out across open ground towards Dudley over fields that had once been farmland around Netherton Hall, until coal was mined, leaving only waste by the end of the nineteenth century. Blackbrook Road continued as a track across the valley and linked Netherton to Woodside, another industrial suburb of Dudley with much in common with Netherton. The two communities are now united in the task of regeneration, although no longer linked by this track or any other! *(Dudley Archives)*

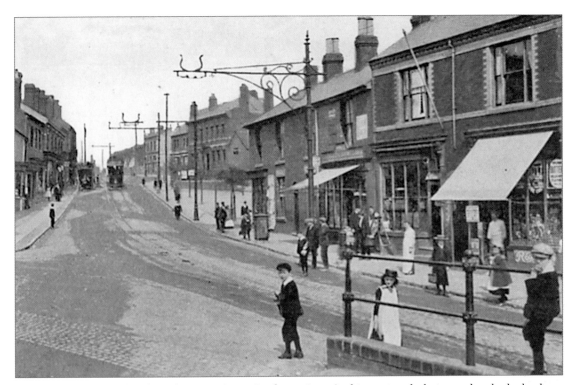

Standing in the middle of Castle Street (now Castleton Street), this postcard photographer looks back up the main road towards the crest of the hill where High Street enters the centre of Netherton and bends to become Halesowen Road. Children in Edwardian clothes and trams passing by on the Dudley–Cradley Heath service set the historical scene. The buildings relate well to what we can see at this spot today but the ambience has totally changed. *(Ken Rock)*

The triangle between Northfield Road and High Street can just be glimpsed in the top picture. Here the postcard photographer looks back into this space, once used as the market place. Although the scene dates from about 1910, the buildings across the back of this view are still there today. *(Ken Rock)*

Pat Collins's ERF eight-wheeler, Zo'e, pulls out of Northfield Road, driven by manager Jacky Harvey in 1962. The Wakes ground was between Northfield Road and the Halesowen Road where Knighton Road exists today. The fire station and police houses on the left are Netherton landmarks and are currently being restored. Northfield Road links central Netherton with Windmill End and Darby End. In the distance a coach is parked outside Davenport's garage, opposite the primary schools. *(Roger Mills)*

This is another Edwardian view, looking down Halesowen Road in the 1900s, with the Castle Street railings in the foreground. The old church school and the Junction Inn can be seen in the distance. Davies and the shop next door are now Taylors & Bains Wines (formerly Netherton Wine Stores – see p. 67.) *(Ken Rock Collection)*

The classic view of Netherton. This tinted postcard from Valentine's series must have been a best-seller in 1900s Netherton. A tram from Cradley Heath seems to be heading for Dudley on the single-track section through the town centre. (Loops were provided at regular intervals.) Well-dressed children fill the scene and the buildings look likely to last for ever. Note the Castle pub and Plant's Brewery behind the tram. The tall building on the right (now part of Costcutter) is Reeves, the newsagent. *(Ken Rock Collection)*

The junction with Cradley Road, photographed in 1968. Beyond the Old Swan shops run from Holden's shoe shop down to Cross Street on the Halesowen Road. *(NW)*

In response to the Valentine's postcard reproduced on p. 17, Reeves the local newsagent sold this beautiful card of central Netherton. As well as featuring their own shop on the right, the card shows the tram shelter and the fountain on the left. The latter was moved to the park and is now lost. Once again we see Plant's Brewery in the background. *(Trudi Blair Collection)*

Church Road was the principal thoroughfare off the main road through Netherton, and ran from the centre of town up to the church. Trinity Methodist Chapel on the extreme right was opened in this form in 1913 and the postcard picture was probably taken soon afterwards. From the chapel up to the church the area remained undeveloped on that side of the road until after the First World War. Victoria Street is on the left. *(Ken Rock)*

This is one of the most interesting views of old Netherton available. Taken in about 1900 it shows the legacy of the nineteenth century in a village like Netherton. The late Victorians and early Edwardians had to clean up the landscape of waste tips, colliery banks and industrial dereliction to make way for new houses, roads and other development. In the foreground is Northfield Road, and we are looking across towards the Halesowen Road on the skyline. The sheds of the railway and canal interchange facilities at Withymoor Basin can be seen on the extreme left and on the right are the pit frames of Dudley Wood No. 2 Colliery. The chimneys in the distance belong to Hingley's works on the far side of Primrose Hill. Subsidence was a major problem. *(Dave Whyley/Keith Hodgkins)*

Church Road, with Trinity in the centre of the picture, 1985. The little shop on the right was built by the builder of the 1920s houses on the extreme right. At one stage a Mrs Saint, and then a Mrs Green, ran it. It has now reverted to domestic use. *(NW)*

As the Halesowen Road left central Netherton it passed the hamlet of Primrose Hill on the right (North Street and Chapel Street) and the Withymoor railway/canal yard on the left, before reaching Bishton's Bridge. This picture looks across the bridge and the Dudley No. 2 Canal towards Danks of Netherton. This site is being developed for canalside housing in 2006. On the extreme left is the junction between the main canal and the entrance to the Withymoor Basin. Beyond Bishton's Bridge the Halesowen Road passes a crossroads at which Cole Street leads to Darby End and Saltwells Road to Dudley Wood. *(Keith Hodgkins)*

A Primrose Hill chapel parade halts in Saltwells Road, *c.* 1950. The houses in the background were still new, and reflect the massive wave of council-house building that spread across the fields and wastes of Dudley Wood just after the Second World War, in this southernmost corner of Netherton. *(Joe Guest)*

At the junction of Dudley Wood Road and Quarry Road was the old hamlet of Dudley Wood, in the remote south-west corner of Netherton, and closer to Cradley Heath. Many pits of the Saltwells Colliery group had caused subsidence. This picture of *c.* 1905 shows that the shop on the corner had survived relatively well, but the houses along Dudley Wood Road had really been twisted. *(Keith Hodgkins)*

The effects of subsidence were still evident in Dudley Wood Road, and were frequently commented on by visitors to the Speedway Track on the opposite side of the road as late as 1974. *(Keith Hodgkins)*

The Boys' Brigade march through New Village in a St John's Sunday School Anniversary parade, 9 June 1964. 'New Village' was set out in the late nineteenth century to provide a location for houses to replace those in Mushroom Green and Dudley Wood. New Village itself fared no better and was buried under a wave of later housing. *(Jeff Parkes)*

From Dudley Wood, Quarry Road leads to Mushroom Green, a small industrial hamlet in which people 'squatted' on the Earl of Dudley's land from the beginning of the nineteenth century onwards. Conservation Area status has protected this area since the 1970s and its surviving chainshop is preserved as an outpost of the Black Country Living Museum. This 2005 picture captures the 'feel' of Mushroom Green. *(NW)*

2
Filling the Gaps &
Exploring the Fringes

Having traversed Netherton on the turnpike road, and taken the Saltwells Road out to Dudley Wood and Mushroom Green, we now have to explore some of the gaps and take a circular tour around the fringes of Netherton.

As we finished the first part of our journey in Mushroom Green, it makes sense to begin our circular tour from there. Travelling up the western frontier of Netherton takes us through Saltwells Woods, past Doulton's Clay Pit, up to the reservoir (the 'rezzer'), round the hill on which the church stands, across Blackbrook Road and across the fiery holes between Netherton Hill and Cinder Bank. Exploring the eastern flank of Netherton would take us from Baptist End, down the old Bumble Hole Road, (now known more respectably as St Peter's Road), to Windmill End, and then Darby End and back to the Halesowen Road just south of Bishton's Bridge.

Doulton's Clay Pit, last worked in about 1947, and photographed in the 1980s, has now become a site of great geological and natural history interest. Clay was extracted here and carried up to the canal via a rope-worked inclined plane or 'tub line'. The clay was used by Doulton's at their pipe works just outside Netherton. Immediately north of the clay pit is Netherton Reservoir. *(NHG)*

Water skiing on Netherton Reservoir, 1970s. The reservoir, sometimes also known as Lodge Farm Reservoir, was created by the Dudley Canal Company in 1838, at the same time that this portion of the canal was slightly realigned. Beyond the reservoir is the Knowle Hill Road estate, behind which there is yet another marl hole or clay pit, which has been levelled to create a hidden playing field. St Andrew's parish church dominates the skyline. *(George Pearson)*

This postcard view looks back across the reservoir in the opposite direction. Houses on the top of the Yew Tree Hills can be seen on the left and the chimney and engine-house associated with Doulton's tub line are on the right. *(Dave Whyley)*

The Netherton Reservoir was transferred from British Waterways to Dudley Council in 1966, and on 6 June 1970 was given a gala opening as the home of Dudley Water Ski and Yachting Club.

Dudley Water Ski and Yachting Club
GALA OPENING
Netherton Reservoir, Saturday, 6th June
Commencing 2 p.m.

Water Ski and Sailing Display
featuring
PAM HORTON
English Ski Ballet Star from the famous
Cypress Gardens Shows, Florida.

To be opened by
NOELE GORDON
(T/V Personality)
Assisted by HIS WORSHIP THE MAYOR OF DUDLEY

PROGRAMME — ONE SHILLING

The original Lodge Farm was to the west of Doulton's tub line, in the valley of the Black Brook. After the Second World War the Lodge Farm Estate was built, and is seen here nestling below Highbridge Road. Until the war Highbridge Road had halted at Brewin's Bridge, from which a footpath extended alongside the reservoir. The road was extended right down to Hurst Lane to provide access to the estate. It now forms a secondary route to the Merry Hill Shopping Centre. When this picture was taken in the 1980s, looking across to the Levels at Round Oak, the Merry Hill complex was still being built. *(NHG)*

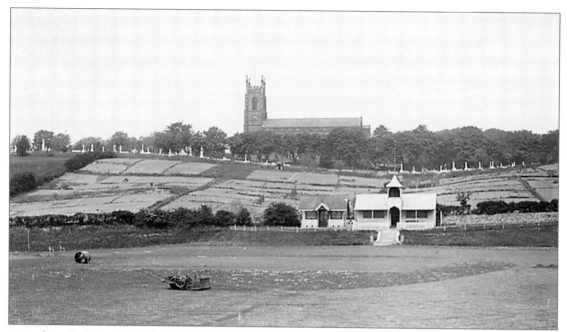

Ascending Netherton Hill from Lodge Farm, and crossing the canal, one comes to Netherton Cricket Club. The club has occupied this site since 1879, when it was presented with its grand pagoda-roofed corrugated-iron pavilion. This picture looks across allotments behind the cricket ground straight into the churchyard. Today this area is occupied by Yew Tree Primary School. *(Erena Little)*

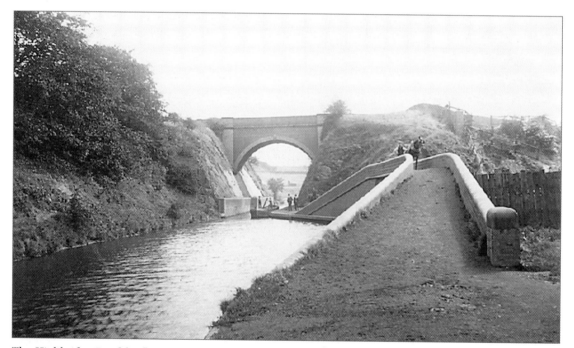

The Highbridge Road bridge seen from the canal. It is also known as Sounding Bridge, and it replaced a short tunnel known as Brewin's Tunnel in the 1850s. (Thomas Brewin was a canal engineer.) On the right the towpath bridge spans the entrance to a basin which served the upper end of the tub line from Doulton's clay pit. *(Ken Rock Collection)*

If one climbs Netherton Hill (see opposite), traverses the churchyard and starts the descent of the other side of the hill, one comes across the Fiery Holes footpath. It follows the side of the churchyard, passes the end of Crescent Road and crosses Blackbrook Road (see p. 14) at this gate. The fields, seen here in 2005, were pit banks and wasteland until fifty years ago. It is possible to descend to the site of Hall Lane Farm, associated with Netherton Hall. One can then make one's way to Cinder Bank. Top Church and Dudley are on the skyline. *(NW)*

To descend from Cinder Bank into Baptist End on the eastern flank of Netherton it is best to take Swan Street (see p. 12). The descent is even more dramatic via Prince Street and Round Street at the back of the Mission. Here a People's Mission parade in 1949 is climbing the steep unmade section of Round Street. The railway embankment is in the background and new houses in Bank Road. *(Harry Rose)*

The railway embankment seen in the picture at the foot of p. 27 carried the freight-only branch to Netherton Goods Depot (see p. 40) and it is seen here continuing past the lower perimeter of the park, while football proceeds in the foreground. Beyond the railway we can glimpse the prefabs in St Paul's Road in this 1949 picture. From this side of Netherton there are good views across to the Rowley Hills. *(Harry Rose)*

Some of the prefabs in St Paul's Road were still standing when this picture was taken in 1989 but they have now been replaced. Prefabs were built after the Second World War at various locations in Netherton including Hockley Lane, and on Lodge Farm. St Paul's Road ran into Bumble Hole Road, now St Peter's Road, leading to Windmill End and Darby End. *(NHG)*

Windmill End was a self-contained hamlet on the eastern edge of Netherton which had grown up to serve local pits and ironworks. It was surrounded by canals and at one time there was no direct road access from Netherton, although it had its own railway station (see p. 40). This 1965 view from the canal embankment looks across the hamlet towards Doulton's works and the Rowley Hills. *(Dudley Archives/Bill Massey)*

Viewed from the railway bridge that carried the line over Vale Road/Springfield and facing the junction of Windmill End with Vale Road, this is Windmill End hamlet in 1965, just at the time when new roads and houses were about to transform the area. Eventually the huge railway embankment on the right would be swept away. *(Dudley Archives/Bill Massey)*

This 1961 view from the top of a pit bank at the end of Stanhope Street shows Withymoor Road passing the watercress beds in the foreground and Darby End Halt in the background, with Doulton's works beyond. Building the railway embankment caused havoc with the course of the Mousesweet Brook, which was Netherton's eastern boundary. *(Dudley Archives)*

Stanhope Street itself in 1961 showing the pit-bank on which the photographer had stood to take the photograph at the top of this page. The houses looked out across what had once been the watercress beds watered by the brook. *(Dudley Archives)*

From Withymoor Road the view of Stanhope Street has changed little over the years in this direction. The road on the right is Stafford Street and the houses in Stanhope Street were sometimes known as Stafford Terrace. All this is a reference to the old county boundary between Staffordshire and Worcestershire (Detached), defined by the Mousesweet Brook. *(NW)*

Darby End extends from the boundary defined above across to Cole Street, and was once another fairly self-contained hamlet and hotbed of Methodism. The inhabitants (the 'Derby Hands') were thought to have come from Derbyshire and that is how the area acquired its name. This street was called Belper Row to reinforce the legend, and this 1961 view shows it in its modernised form. Older and more interesting housing is still to be found round the corner in Gill Street. *(Dudley Archives/Bill Massey)*

Having completed a circular photographic tour of the fringes of Netherton, we need to fill in a few gaps. The area to the west of Cradley Road was barely developed at the beginning of the twentieth century. Griffin Street, seen here in 1961, was the southernmost residential development of nineteenth-century Netherton and it stopped level with the houses in the middle distance of this picture. Later it was extended to Marriot Road and waves of housing development followed. *(Dudley Archives/Bill Massey)*

Marriot Road, seen here in 1962, was built in the twentieth century, leaving Church Road opposite St Andrew's Street and then curving to follow an existing track down to the Cradley Road, just behind the Lloyd's Proving House. It was named after St Andrew's vicar of forty-five years: the Revd S.J. Marriot. Properties on both sides of the road then belonged to Clydesdale Stampings. The roof of Primrose Hill Chapel is visible on the skyline. *(Dudley Archives/Bill Massey)*

Another vast area of Netherton is the Yew Tree Hills. Seen here in the 1900s it is a vast open space, quarried on its western flank by marl holes. On the left is Hockley Lane, which took explorers from Church Road up to the Yew Tree public house in the distance. The road was improved and, after the war, prefabs were put up here until more permanent houses were built. *(Dudley Archives)*

Superb views in several directions are obtained from the Yew Tree Hills. This scene is taken from the point where the road turns back from the ridge and descends towards Marriot Road. Housing on the estates on both sides of Saltwells Road can be seen, as well as Old Hill and Halesowen, with the Clent Hills on the horizon. *(NW)*

Hockley Lane leads you from Church Road up to the heights of the Yew Tree Hills and relatively modern housing. The turning on the other side of Church Road is Bell Street, which plunges you back into Victorian Netherton. Both Bell Road and Church Road contain many fine houses and this is Jubilee Cottage in Bell Road – obviously built in 1897. Bell Road itself was so named to commemorate the installation of the church's bells in 1871, which were augmented in 1897. *(NHG)*

King Street, now known as Kingsley Street, is home to this old blue-brick house bearing a plaque with a cryptic message dated August 1865, and beyond is Round's Bakery building of 1931, now the home of Autocycle Engineering. Behind this is Alpha Bearings. *(NW)*

3
Transport

Transport has played a big part in the history of Netherton. The construction of the Dudley–Halesowen–Bromsgrove turnpike road was what put Netherton on the map. At about the same time canals were arriving to facilitate the industrial growth of the area. Many of the major works were built with a view to being served by the canal. Eventually Netherton was completely surrounded by canal!

When the Oxford, Worcester & Wolverhampton Railway pushed its way northwards from Stourbridge to Dudley in 1852 it missed Netherton but concealed the fact by creating a station called 'Netherton' well to the south of the tunnel which took the line through to Dudley station. The station had to be moved northwards and re-christened Dudley South Side and Netherton when the junction was created in the 1870s to provide access to the Bumble Hole Line, which was really Netherton's railway, although it passed along the eastern boundary of the town while keeping to the valley of the Mousesweet Brook. A 'goods traffic only' branch from Baptist End to Withymoor Basin was extremely important.

Residential development in Netherton at the end of the nineteenth century was stimulated by the electric tramway, and twentieth-century housing development prompted the Midland Red company to provide more bus services to serve Netherton.

A Midland Red Guy Arab double decker on the D9 service turned over in Marriot Road, 12 May 1956. Twelve people were hurt and were taken to Dudley Guest Hospital. *(Dudley Archives)*

The Dudley No. 2 Canal was authorised in 1793 to build an 11-mile stretch of waterway from Parkhead Basin on the Dudley Canal to Selly Oak on the Worcester & Birmingham Canal, via Netherton, Halesowen and the Lapal Tunnel. It opened on 28 May 1798. This revived the collieries around Netherton and stimulated the construction of works, basins and wharves. Here we see Doulton's wharf, near the Sounding Bridge and at the summit of their tub line, in about 1905. *Below:* Hingley's wharves and pig iron arriving from Old Hill. *(NHG)*

The Dudley No. 2 was a contour canal. Having circled Netherton, it had to circle the Bumble Hole to reach the far side of the valley of the Mousesweet Brook. The horseshoe bend in the canal was cut off when the Netherton Tunnel was opened in 1858 but remained in use for Windmill End Boilerworks and several boatyards. It is now cut back to Harris's Bumble Hole Boatyard, where the crane has dominated the scene until recent times. In 1948 the last boat to be built by Jack Harris was supplied to Stewarts & Lloyds at Coombes Wood. *(Peter Harris)*

Later the Bumble Hole Boatyard was run by R. Chater, who began to construct the windmill captured in this photograph, perhaps in memory of another folly, Zaiah's Castle, which stood nearby. In the background is the roof of the Boat public house on St Peter's Road (see p. 87). In the mid-1980s a 'fun pub' called the Willows operated in the boatyard itself. *(NHG)*

The Netherton Tunnel, opened on 20 August 1858, is another of Netherton's claims to fame, giving direct access from the Dudley No. 2 Canal to the rest of the Birmingham Canal Navigation's system at Tividale, 3,027 yards away. It is a modern 'wide' tunnel with a towpath on each side. Subsidence was a problem in 1902 and again in the 1980s. Both pictures were taken on 18 April 1984 when Trevor Luckcuck of the British Waterways Board reopened the canal and tunnel after restoration work. *(Keith Hodgkins)*

Windmill End still lives up to the romance of its name. Spoil heaps, marl holes, canals, railway trackbeds, bridges and a Visitors' Centre, to what has become a conservation area, await the explorer. In the early 1960s, when this picture was taken, mainline trains were sometimes diverted via the Bumble Hole Line which added to the interest. All trace of the railway line has now virtually disappeared. The canal finger-post has been replaced. *(W. Boyd)*

The Bumble Hole Line on its way from Dudley to Old Hill entered Netherton at Baptist End Halt, seen here on 31 August 1962 as the single-car diesel train makes its way to Dudley. In the background is Windmill End Junction and the divergence of the branch to Withymoor Basin. *(P.J. Shoesmith)*

Windmill End Halt and Darby End Halt were just within the boundaries of Netherton, although Windmill End, seen here, had been a full-blown station when the line opened in 1878. Ex-GWR 0–6–0 PT No. 6424 pauses at Windmill End Halt just before the service was finally withdrawn on 13 June 1964. *(NW)*

Seen from Northfield Road, looking towards Halesowen Road, this view shows the expanse of the goods yard at Withymoor Basin, opened March 1879, closed July 1965. *(NW)*

There were several coach operators that were well known in Netherton, including Holden's, Corbett's, and Davenport's, among others. One of Holden's Luxury Radio Coaches, a 1935 Leyland Cub with Brush-built rear-entrance bodywork, is seen here with Bill Holden, wearing his PSV badge, fourth from left, with his sons Terrence and Ron in front of him. The business began in Cradley Road and moved to Baptist End Road. Bill's sons sold the coaching side of the business in 1952 to Corbett's but kept the taxis and garage going until 1985. *(Joyce Holden)*

Davenport's Netherton 'Depot' on 18 July 1966. Two Duple-bodied Bedford coaches are nestling alongside the washing. Davenport's were based in Cinder Bank and operated from about 1929 to May 1976 when their vehicles were sold to Prospect Coaches of the Lye. Davenport's eventually used a garage on Northfield Road, now used by Black Country Tours. *(John Tennent)*

Fred Corbett was also a coach operator, having taken over from J. Smith & Co. of Cinder Bank (see p. 3) at the end of the Second World War. However, Fred became better known as a garage proprietor and car dealer – selling Austin, Morris, Riley and Wolseley cars. In the mid-1950s Fred Corbett opened the new showroom seen on the right. *(Doris Corbett Collection)*

Surrounded by Austin Cambridges, the staff at Fred Corbett's toast the new models. *Left to right:* unknown in beret, Ron Corbett (head of car sales), Jack Harris, three office staff, George Corbett in white coat (manager), Ivy Harris (née Corbett), Mrs Fred Corbett, Betty Corbett (blurred), Doris Corbett, and Fred Corbett (managing director). *(Doris Corbett Collection)*

4
Netherton at Work

Netherton was turned from a village on the outskirts of Dudley into an urban community with its own identity by industrialisation and the population explosion that followed. The Netherton of 1900 is portrayed by the Ordnance Survey map recently published in the Alan Godfrey series and it shows an area that is already a vast exhausted coalfield. Disused pits and their spoil heaps abound. Large 'works' are found along the banks of the Dudley No. 2 Canal, including at least two sets of blast furnaces. In our imagination we have to construct a picture of Netherton crowded with colliers, iron-makers and iron-workers – making everything from huge anchors and chains, to small items like edge tools and nails.

Huge works like Danks, Hingley's, and Barnsley's have gone, but in some cases modern industrial estates occupy their sites. These estates and the large number of small businesses scattered all over Netherton are a reminder that Netherton was, and is, an industrial town. However, one thing that may have changed is that the workforce is not so 'local'.

These pictures illustrate a time when Netherton people worked in Netherton's industries.

A Valentine's postcard of the 1900s captures the atmosphere of a Black Country ironworks just as they were disappearing from the Netherton area. These were Pearson's furnaces, a company that supplied a great deal of pig-iron to Hingley's. There were two ironworks in Netherton that survived into the twentieth century: one seen here, just off Northfield Road, and the 'old' furnaces close to Peartree Lane. (*Ken Rock*)

Netherton furnaces, 1935. The furnace on the left had been little altered since it was built in the 1850s; the one on the right had been slightly 'modernised'. The entire plant, which had produced high-quality foundry pig-iron, came to the end of its life in 1946. These furnaces were part of Glazebrook's works on Peartree Lane. *(The late W.V.K. Gale)*

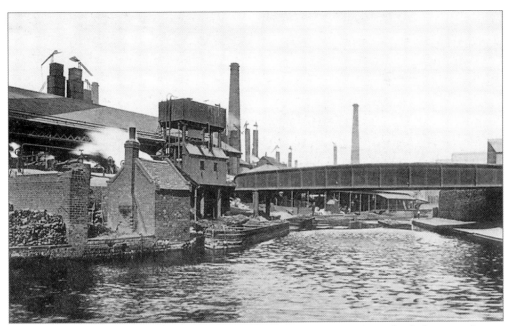

This 1900s Valentine's postcard once again captures the essence of canal-side heavy industry. At this point the Dudley No. 2 Canal is passing the huge works belonging to Noah Hingley & Sons. The works grew up during the mid-nineteenth century and became well known for the production of anchors and anchor chain, as well as hooks, boilers, and a variety of iron forgings. It was a major local employer – particularly in the Primrose Hill area close to the works. *(Ken Rock)*

Another 1900s postcard features Hingley's anchor for the *Titanic* awaiting despatch, loaded on to a LNWR dray. Although raw materials seem to have been brought in to Hingley's by canal, finished products seem to have left by rail, entailing a road journey to the railhead. *(Ken Rock)*

The most famous Netherton picture of all time shows the departure of the anchor for the *Titanic* on 1 May 1911, forged by Hingley's. Twenty horses were attached to the dray carrying the 16-ton anchor but folklore exists to suggest that this was more than actually necessary, although it did have to be pulled over the hill to the LNWR Goods station in Tipton Road, Dudley. *(Ken Rock)*

Finishing a large link in Hingley's chain and anchor department in the 1930s. *(NHG)*

A Davy 800-ton hydraulic press worked in the Drop Forging and Stamping Department at
Hingley's, and this carefully composed 1930s photograph portrays the relationship between
men, machines and the metal they bashed. Hingley's, in the form of Wright Hingley Ltd,
modernised after the war and developed expertise in forging non-ferrous metals, but did not
survive the 1980s de-industrialisation of the region. *(NHG)*

Hingley's own testing shop, seen here, was only a stone's throw from Lloyd's Proving House on the other side of Cradley Road. It too was served by the Dudley No. 2 Canal. *(NHG)*

Lloyd's Proving House seen from the Dudley No. 2 Canal in July 1975 – once a busy wharf where chain was brought to be tested and then despatched. Part of the building is still used by a steel stockholder today. *(Keith Hodgkins)*

Hingley's had their own iron-making facilities in Old Hill, and owned Saltwells Colliery, which was made up of a number of pits in Netherton and Quarry Bank. *(Dave Whyley)*

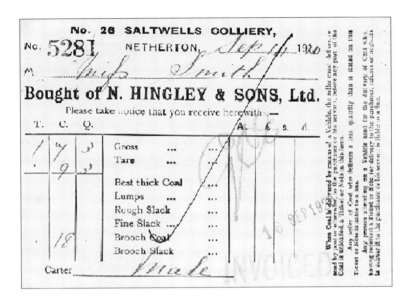

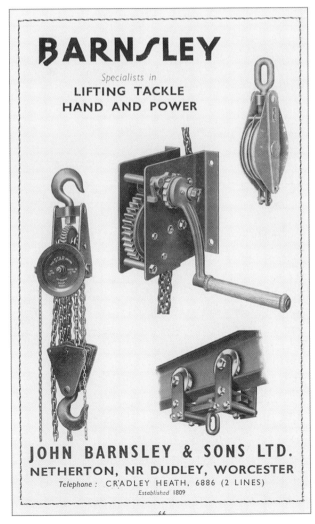

John Barnsley & Sons was established in 1809 when the firm started manufacturing Jews' harps. Later they developed a specialism in the manufacture of pulley blocks, chains and lifting equipment. By the time the firm was celebrating its centenary in 1959, they described themselves as 'Crane & Hoist Engineers' and were able to supply overhead cranes capable of lifting 50 tons. The advert seen here dates from the 1950s. *(NHG)*

John Barnsley & Co. built a large works
known as the Netherton Foundry at the
corner of Saltwells Road and Cradley Road.
Above: a glazing firm now uses Barnsley's
works on Cradley Road. *(Fred Emery)*
Right: a supermarket now occupies the
foundry building site. *(Fred Emery)*
Below: A typical Black Country foundry
scene at John Barnsley's in the 1960s.
(Joe Guest)

Above: An overhead crane platform in the process of construction at John Barnsley's in the 1960s. *Below:* a publicity photograph of the finished overhead crane. *(Both pictures Joe Guest)*

Danks of Netherton were established in 1840 and were manufacturers of boilers. The completion of a boiler and preparation for despatch also seems to have been recognised as a photo-opportunity. *(Peter Glews)*

A Midland Road Services tractor unit and trailer poses for the camera in the 1930s with a pressure vessel completed by Danks for delivery to a Dunlop tyre factory. *(NHG)*

What a wonderful portrait of part of the workforce at Danks. Was cap-wearing compulsory before the Second World War? *(Wesley Garratt)*

Not far from Danks were George Bissell & Sons, Coopers, where once more the workers seem keen to pose for a picture in their hats. This photograph was taken on their Halesowen Road premises in about 1925. *(Alma Guest)*

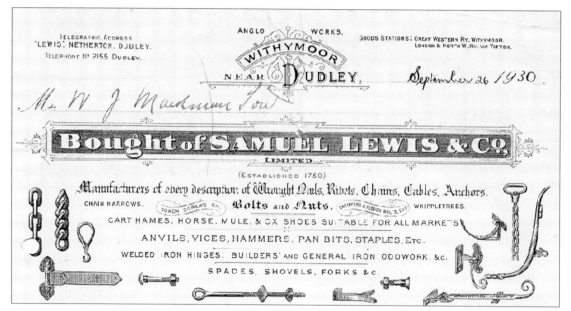

Samuel Lewis & Co. of Withymoor were established in 1750, making them one of the oldest firms in the area. They manufactured chains, bolts, nuts, anvils, hammers, shovels and forks. *(Letterhead supplied by Dave Whyley)*

Swindell & Co. were near neighbours of Samuel Lewis and made very much the same range of products from a factory next door to the Providence Chapel in Northfield Road. Here the employees display a variety of products in about 1910. For example, George Roberts is standing fourth from left with his thumb tucked into the armhole of his waistcoat while he displays a hay knife – one of the edge tools in which he specialised. *(George Roberts Jnr)*

Staff and employees at Griffiths Chainworks, Mushroom Green, 1939. *(Jeff Parkes)*

A chainshop has been preserved at Mushroom Green so that present and future generations can appreciate the skills involved in making hand-made chain. The area had first attracted nail-makers, who later graduated to chain-making, only to see that become mechanised. Mick Bradney demonstrates the task in recent times. *(NW)*

Another major industrial area in Netherton, but right on the boundary with Dudley, is a site once occupied by M. & W. Grazebrook Ltd, seen in the centre of this aerial photograph of *c.* 1950. Netherton's boundary comes up the centre of the Dudley No. 2 Canal on the right and turns up the centre of Pear Tree Lane to leave to the left. Across the top of the picture is Cinder Bank. On the left is Grazebrook's new foundry building, built in 1949. The arc-roofed building is part of the tank wagon-building plant and it is just possible to make out their internal rail network. *(NHG)*

The 0–4–0 ST 'Grazebrook No. 2' with a mild steel welded tank about to leave the works in 1949. The locomotive was built by Peckett of Bristol in 1938 and worked at Grazebrook's until 1962. *(NHG)*

The Grazebrook family came to the Black Country in the seventeenth century and over the next hundred years they acquired mills, collieries and a glassworks. In 1800 a member of the fourth generation established a business in Netherton by taking over some existing pits and a blast furnace. They expanded their range of metal-working while continuing to produce their own pig-iron, ever increasing their reputation as heavy engineers. As can be seen above, fabrication became increasingly important, and both before and after the war there was frequent modernisation of the plant – as can be seen below, as workers pose between new and mightier presses. *(NHG)*

A tractor unit belonging to Wynn's of Newport prepares to leave Netherton with a huge pressure vessel bound for Albright & Wilson's Kirkby works, *c.* 1950. Making such vessels enabled the company to diversify into making railway tank wagons both for use in the UK and abroad. Delivery was simplified by the fact that Grazebrook's had an internal rail system linked to the main railway system at Blowers Green. *(NHG)*

John Thompson was another local boilermaker, and in the nineteenth century the business used the Windmill Boilerworks by the Bumble Hole at Windmill End. The firm then relocated to Peartree Lane and eventually became Thompson Horsley as part of the Horsley Piggott company, later Clarke Chapman. This appears to be a postwar picture when presumably 'horse power' was being used just to move products around the factory. *(Keith Hodgkins)*

Everyone seems wrapped up one Christmas at Freeman's Boat Dock on Bumble Hole Road. On the right are Richard Roberts and Wilfrid Freeman. As well as boat repairs the firm undertook coffin manufacture, and eventually became funeral directors. *(Brian Roberts)*

Young women working at Little's shoe factory, Hill Street, 1930s. *(Erena Little)*

William Little was born in Netherton in 1826 and was deterred from working in the pits by a couple of early accidents. Instead he joined an uncle in a boot and shoe repair business. In about 1850 he established his own boot-making business which grew rapidly. A Netherton man known as 'Lord' Hartshorne walked from Land's End to John O'Groats using two pairs of Little's boots in about 1900 and sales rocketed. William Little died in 1906, but a few years later the next generation started adding sports shoes to the company's range. In the 1960s, John Little, the fourth generation and a Moseley Rugby Club captain, really pushed the company further into producing top-quality sports shoes and introduced the Winit brand. Winit sports boots and shoes became a great success and succeeded in exporting a Netherton product all round the world. *(Erena Little)*

Many sportsmen gave their endorsement to Winit footwear. In this early 1980s picture we see Bob Willis, England cricketer and bowler, with Taff Hughes, who joined Little's as a sales rep and went on to become sales director. A boot was specially designed by Little's to take the strain on a bowler's ankle and knee joints – and thus extend a cricketer's career. The design team in the Hill Street factory were both innovative and inventive and this made the Winit brand a success. The firm was bought out in 1988 and left Netherton for Dudley, and the Hill Street factory site still awaits redevelopment. *(Erena Little)*

Mr J. Talbot was typical of the long-serving workforce at Little's shoe factory. He joined the firm in 1899 as an experienced 26-year-old boot-maker, and in 1950 when the firm was celebrating its centenary he had completed fifty-one years' service. He was 78 years old when this picture was taken! He was working at the factory when 'Lord' Hartshorne completed his famous walk in Little's boots, and Mr Talbot was responsible for preparing a supply of paper socks, which 'Lord' Hartshorne wore inside his boots. *(Erena Little)*

John Little was a keen photographer. He took these pictures, two from a whole series, of his own workforce to illustrate the 1950 centenary booklet *A Century of Boot Making*. *(Erena Little)*

By the 1980s many of Netherton's large 'works' were being vacated, stripped of machinery, and then demolished. This is the scene at Hingley's former works in July 1989. The Washington Centre now provides modern industrial estate facilities on the site. On the other side of Halesowen Road, canal-side housing occupies the Danks' factory site. *(NW)*

5
Going to the Shops

Everyone who passes through Netherton can claim to know its shops, but shops are always changing hands and the self-contained world of Netherton that existed fifty years ago when your every shopping need could be satisfied without needing to travel further afield has gradually been replaced with the modern world of takeaways, the odd supermarket or two, and a less satisfactory variety of services. Shops that had been family businesses run by Netherton people have disappeared, and the streetscape created by those shops has been disfigured. How can the authorities have let it become such a mess?

It is also a mistake to think that Netherton's shops were simply those encountered along Cinder Bank, High Street and the Halesowen Road. As the new residential areas were established they were provided with local shops, but photographers are likely to have ignored them. And then there are the interesting curiosities – the 'iron shops' at Darby End, a Wild West store in the centre of Netherton, and little corner shops in unexpected places.

Netherton's most famous shop was H. Emile Doo's pharmacy, seen here at 94 (formerly 358) Halesowen Road in 1968. James Emile Doo qualified as a pharmacist in 1882 and acquired Thomas Perkins's shop at 9 Netherton High Street in 1887. In 1909 he moved the business to 34/5 Halesowen Road. His son Harold Emile Doo, known as Jack, took over his father's business in 1920, and in 1929 he moved the business across the road to No. 358. Jack Doo retired in 1968 and the shop was put up for sale. The premises, however, remained untouched until after his death in 1970. *(Betty Doo Collection)*

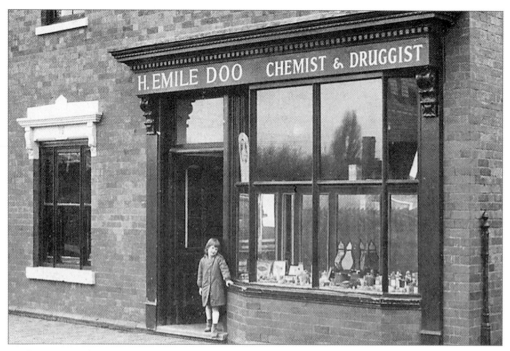

Emile Doo's shop re-created at the Black Country Living Museum. After Mr Doo's death some of the shop fittings and stock were presented by his family to the museum. As the building itself was for sale, the shop had to be replicated at the museum rather than transferred brick by brick. However, Mr Doo had never thrown anything away and volunteers took some time to transfer other treasures to the museum. In 1979 it became possible to transfer the original shop front. On 19 May 1980 Betty Doo was able to reopen her late father's shop at the museum. This picture was taken during 1985. *(NW)*

One of Jack Doo's legendary window displays of the 1950s. *(Betty Doo Collection)*

Netherton post office, *c.* 1904.
Crowds assembled outside the
office in October 1899 to hear
news of the siege of Mafeking
because the office was one of the
first in the area to receive news by
Morse telegraphy. The Netherton
postmaster seen in the centre of
the picture was Mr Fred Homer.
Later the office was run by his
son, Len Homer. Second from
right, front row, is Emily Higgins
who took the Mafeking message
and in 1975 became Dudley's
oldest shopkeeper at her Buffery
Road greengrocery. *(Ray Jones)*

Netherton's post office in the
position in which most people will
remember it, next door to Baker's
Stores. This picture was taken in
1978, just before the Homer family
sold the building and the post
office facility moved to the other
side of the road. *(Keith Hodgkins)*

The post office has now moved to the other side of the road, into premises that were once used by Dudley Co-operative Society. The society expanded from its base in Salop Street, Eve Hill, in the early 1880s and opened its first two branches: here and in Kates Hill. The Halal butchers and Balti takeaway, seen here in 2004, occupy a well-designed blue-brick building – seen again on the opposite page. *(NW)*

Netherton post office seen next door to Grainger's in April 1986. Grainger's were one of a number of well-known local butcher's, most of whom seem to have been related to one another. *(NW)*

The Halesowen Road curves through the centre of Netherton past the shops. Firkin's bakery shop is still there today, but the haberdashery and clothes shop next door has gone. Firkin's shop front has been modernised, retaining the blue corporate colours. The company, based in West Bromwich, acquired shops in this area by taking over Robinson's. This picture dates from 1986. *(NW)*

The Netherton Wine Stores at 77 Halesowen Road is seen here in 1986. Black vitrolite as a fascia and script-based lettering became very fashionable in the 1930s and this would have been quite a classy 'modern' addition to Netherton's shopping scene. It is now Bains Wines, and this frontage has been replaced. *(NW)*

Scriven's butcher's shop dominates the corner of Castle Street in this 1960s view of the other side of Netherton's main thoroughfare. Scriven's simply leased the ground floor of this building. Castle Street has since been renamed Castleton Street, and Win's greengrocer's shop occupied the corner for a few years. *(Dudley Archives)*

Win's greengrocer's, photographed in 1986, on the corner of Castle Street and St John's Street, 'Win' being Winston Churchill. At one time the premises were known as Cole's, and Mr Cole delivered milk locally from the shop. Later the shop was leased by Scriven's, who put this vitrolite frontage on the building (see above). It is now boarded up. *(NW)*

These are the shops seen from the triangle between Halesowen Road and Northfield Road in 1961. This had once been a market place – see p. 15. Baker's shop can be seen with its blind drawn down. To the left of Baker's is Rhodes' fish and chip shop – later incorporated into Baker's (see below). To the right of Baker's is the original post office and its entry. Behind the tree was Harry Shaw's, a printer. *(Dudley Archives)*

Baker's Stores, known to everyone as 'Ernie Baker's shop', photographed in 1986. The shop's address was originally 44 High Street, reminding us that the main road was not Halesowen Road until curving southwards. The shop was originally run by Nancy and Ernie Baker and then by their daughter Sheila and her husband, John Mellor. It closed in 2001. *(NW)*

Sheila and John Mellor behind the counter of the shop always remembered as Ernie Baker's shop, seen in the 1980s. It was typical of Dudley and Netherton that Baker's should be grocers! *(Sheila Baker Collection)*

The old post office run by Len Homer, and separated from Baker's by an entry, became the Ranch House in October 1978, with an official opening on 3 March 1979. This picture was taken in 1986 before line-dancing and the popularity of country and western music had conditioned us to think that such a shop was 'usual' rather than 'specialised'. *(NW)*

Shops also continued a short way down one side of Cradley Road – opposite the Junction Inn, seen here in 1968. This row included Bob Carpenter's butcher's shop, a hairdresser, and another butcher's shop! In 1939 there were thirty-nine butchers trading in the Netherton area. *(NW)*

Bob Carpenter in his Cradley Road shop in the 1950s. Bob was born in 1916 and grew up in a family of shopkeepers and butchers. He worked at Pharoah Adams's shop while still at school, and later worked for Sam Grainger, his uncle. He acquired a shop in Dudley Wood about 1935, and the one in Cradley Road in about 1937. While Bob was on RAF service in the war, the family kept the shop going and Bob ran the shop right up until 1981. *(Bob Carpenter Collection)*

In 1981, when Bob Carpenter retired, he was able to sell the shop to Gary Flavell, who still runs the shop today. In April 2005 89-year-old Bob was able to visit his old shop in Cradley Road to see how it was progressing. Sadly, he died in August of that year. *(NW)*

April 2005. Left to right: Kevin Wright, June Whitehouse, Bob Carpenter and Gary Flavell in Bob's old shop in Cradley Road, now improved and extended by Gary. When Bob first worked in Cradley Road (at Pharoah Adams's), there was no running water supplied to these shops – he had to fetch water from Plant's Brewery. Cattle had to be driven from Hagley Mart to Darby End to be slaughtered at Hotchkiss's. *(NW)*

Reeves's shop at 9 Halesowen Road: Newsagents, Tobacconists, Confectionery, Stationery and Fancy Goods. The business was founded by Mrs Hannah Reeves. She died in 1900 and left the shop to her son Thomas James Reeves. To take over the business he had to give up his job as a schoolmaster. After his death in 1946, his widow carried it on until her death. Once again it passed to the son: Tom Reeves Jnr. History repeated itself: Tom Reeves Jnr died in 1955 and his widow continued to run the shop until her retirement in 1966. The business was then sold – having been in the family for over 100 years. As the leading local newsagent, Reeves produced a series of Netherton postcards. Tom Snr stands in the doorway of his shop before the Second World War. Note the Stephens' Ink enamel sign in the form of a thermometer and the board used for advertising Davenport's coach trips. *(Trudi Blair Collection)*

On the right Dolly Reeves, with her daughter Trudi Blair, behind the counter at Reeves's, *c.* 1964. *(Trudi Blair Collection)*

Allan's Shopping Centre, photographed in the 1980s, continues the great tradition of being the kind of shop that sells everything, as opposed to the old shops of Netherton that were generally rather specialised. It occupies a site that was once Holden's shoe shop. Holden's suffered a fire, and Allan opened on the site in the early 1970s. *(NHG)*

Cinder Bank, and its continuation into High Street, was also once well supplied with shops of all kinds. In this 1989 picture it can be seen how they often occupied the ground floor of quite large buildings – reflecting the confidence in the 1890s and 1900s with which people built substantial houses and shops along the tram route. *(NW)*

The 'Tin Shops' of Darby End. Along a line from Birch Coppice to Darby End there seems to have been desire to erect buildings in corrugated iron. (Birch Coppice Chapel, the Iron Schools, and these shops.) It may be that there are geological as well as economic reasons for this. This shop was built in the 1900s and was run for about twenty years by Joseph Reid, then by Elijah Darby, as a grocery from the Oak Street entrance and as an off-licence from the Cole Street one, and coal from the yard. John Faulkner took over from Elijah Darby and then Geoff Roberts from 1970 to 1982. In this 1986 picture it is Essdee's Stores. *(NW)*

The tin shop on the corner of Northfield Road was originally Scriven's, then Les and Nellie Clarke's. *(Margaret Attwood)*

Local shops were also provided on the large housing estates built around the fringes of Netherton. Some have survived, as in Lodge Farm, others have closed, as in Knowle Hill. The Saltwells estates, on either side of Saltwells Road, have provided a larger customer base. Even so, here we see different styles of shop provision – next door to each other on Saltwells Road, photographed in the 1980s. The small general store in an old building, below, contrasts with the modernity of Cox's tobacconists. *(NHG. Ian Layton/Bill Harris)*

6
Down the Pub

There is no doubt that Netherton has had its fair share of public houses. One in particular has become famous: the Old Swan, right in the centre of the township. It was not the only pub in Netherton that brewed its own beer, and this interest in brewing created several small local breweries. But no book about Netherton can ignore the story of the Old Swan and the Pardoe family.

Fred Pardoe took the licence of the Old Swan in 1932 and ran the pub for the next thirty years until his death, at the age of 52, in 1952. His widow, Doris Pardoe, took over the business, and became well known as 'Ma Pardoe'. She was a teetotaller who regulated her customers' drinking, but her judgement on running the pub was second to none. Doris carried on until 1980 when ill-health forced her retirement, and the licence was transferred to her son-in-law, Sid Allport.

Doris died in 1984 and during the same year Sid Allport stated that he wanted to retire and that the Old Swan would be up for sale. By then CAMRA – the Campaign for Real Ale – was well organised and was able to help form a company to run the pub in the way that everyone liked. Today it still brings people from all over the world to Netherton.

Fred Pardoe, on the right, outside the Old Swan and his maternal grandfather, Edward Jones, who ran the Station Hotel, Dudley, *c.* 1935. *(Erena Little)*

On entering the Old Swan newcomers were struck by the traditional atmosphere of a Black Country pub plus details like the cast-iron stove and its flue, and the enamelled ceiling – seen above, featuring this drawing. *(Erena Little)*

In recent years the Old Swan has been extended, while the exterior of the original building has been preserved, as seen in this 1998 picture. It is currently run by Tim Newey, who doubles as organist at St Andrew's. *(NW)*

Doris and Fred Pardoe of the Old Swan. Fred died in 1952, and the business was then run by Doris, better known as 'Ma Pardoe', and her daughter Brenda. *(Erena Little)*

The long-serving brewer at the Old Swan was George Cooksey, seen here cleaning the casks in May 1982. Before people 'rediscovered' the qualities of home-brewed ale, George was producing one batch a month. In the 1970s this leapt to six times as much. *(Keith Hodgkins)*

Fred Pardoe, left, supported the Netherton Cricket Club, West Bromwich Albion, the Sons of
Rest, the Royal Antediluvian Order of Buffaloes, and the Netherton Homing Society – hence
the pigeons. He was also president of the Dudley Licensed Victuallers Association and is seen
here in about 1948. *(Erena Little)*

Fred Pardoe was also keen to promote darts at the Old Swan and he appears front row left in
this picture of the team, *c.* 1948. *(Erena Little)*

With Fred Pardoe's support the local lodge (3645) of the Royal Ancient Order of Buffaloes ('The Buffs') met at the Old Swan in the 1930s. Fred can be spotted third from left on the front row. Friendly societies thrived in Netherton until the First World War but then began a long decline. *(Erena Little)*

Brenda Pardoe (later wife of Sid Allport) sits in the bar of the Old Swan – transformed for Harvest Festival in aid of the Sons of Rest, *c.* 1938. *(Erena Little)*

The Old Swan should not be confused with the White Swan. The latter, seen here in about 1910, is on the corner of Swan Street and Baptist End Road – perhaps on, or close to, the site of the original Baptist chapel of Baptist End. The landlord at the time was James Roe. The Roe family brewed here between the 1880s and 1939. *(Keith Hodgkins)*

The Junction Inn, at the junction of Cradley Road and Halesowen Road, enjoys a prominent site in central Netherton, but is now the home of Age Concern. *(NW)*

The similarity between these two images reminds us that the townscape of Netherton had developed by Edwardian times then lasted until demolition began to transform the place from the 1960s onwards.

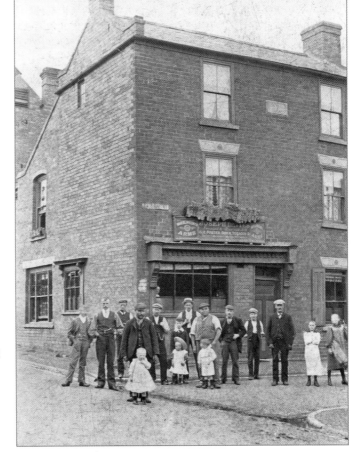

Above: The Wheelwrights Arms in Castleton Street, now Castle Street, and Griffin Street, photographed in 1962, a few years before demolition. *(Dave Whyley)*
Right: The Wheelwrights Arms seen about 1910 when the licensee was Joseph Davies. *(Jeff Parkes)*

Looking down Washington Street towards the Halesowen Road, with the Loyal Washington on the corner. At one time it was a Plant's house, until Plant's Brewery was purchased by Ansell's. The pub was one of several that served the Primrose Hill area and took its name from William Washington, a one-time canal carrier with strong loyalist opinions despite a remote connection to President George Washington – a Republican! *(Jeff Parkes Collection)*

The Bird in Hand, Chapel Street, seen here *c.* 1962, also served the Primrose Hill area. Brewing was carried on here in the nineteenth century by the Onslow family. Although closed in 1970, the building still exists today. *(Dudley Archives)*

The New Inn on the corner of Raybould's Fold and High Street, photographed in 1963 before redevelopment finally swept it away. New flats can now be seen down Raybould's Fold following the demolition of older properties. *(Dudley Archives/Bill Massey)*

At the other end of the railings and raised footpath in High Street, seen starting in the top picture, was the Spread Eagle Hotel. The hotel was photographed in 1963 and subsequently demolished, but the house next door still stands today. *(Dudley Archives/Bill Massey)*

The Royal Exchange in Simms Lane, on the corner of St James Street, 1958. It was a 'standard' Black Country pub with central entrance and bay windows on either side like so many of those seen here. The number of Plant's/Ansell's pubs in the area was a result of the proximity to the Plant's Brewery at the bottom of St John's Street. *(Dudley Archives)*

The Brickmakers Arms, 6 Chapel Street, 1963. *(Dudley Archives/Bill Massey)*

The Red Cow at 38 Belper Row, Darby End, was quite distinctive but its appearance did not save it from demolition. It closed on 14 May 1960 and was not being used as a pub when photographed in 1961. *(Dudley Archives/Bill Massey)*

The Boat Inn in Bumble Hole Road, now St Peter's Road, was another 'standard' double-bay-fronted pub. Although no longer a pub, at least in this case the building has survived. It occupies a narrow site between the Bumble Hole boatyard and the road – hence its name. This photograph dates from 1984. *(Keith Hodgkins)*

The Hope Tavern on the corner of Cinder Bank and Swan Street, seen here in 2001, is still 'going strong'. In 2005 it was taken over by a new landlady, Sharon Wedge. The Hope Tavern acquired notoriety on 24 August 1899 when a gas explosion ripped through the building and three regulars who were playing cards were killed. The rather Edwardian appearance of the building suggests that it may have been rebuilt at that time, but it certainly fits in well with the elegant red-brick buildings of Cinder Bank. *(NW)*

The Miners Arms, St John's Street, 1983. This building is now a construction company's office. *(NW)*

The Britannia Inn, Northfield Road, had a very special role in guarding the entrance and exit to the Wakes Ground, and supplying fresh water to the showmen when the fair came to town. Here we see Pat Collins's Scammell tractor, 'The Major', pulling the loads off the Wakes Ground into Northfield Road in 1962. The pub closed in 1970. *(Roger Mills)*

Another Plant's pub was the Crown Inn at 97 Halesowen Road – not to be confused with the Crown in Hill Street, or the Old Crown at 76 Halesowen Road! *(Keith Hodgkins)*

The Golden Cross, where Cradley Road crosses Saltwells Road, was an old nineteenth-century pub, owned by Round's Brewery, but that was replaced with this large roadhouse by Wolverhampton & Dudley Breweries in 1938. Here it is in 1992. *(Jeff Parkes)*

The Dry Dock, Windmill End, 1998. It is now a popular theme pub with narrowboat bar and canal-inspired decor. The building was originally the Bullfields Hotel and it dominated the Windmill End landscape, towering above its neighbours (see p. 29). Windmill End's other nineteenth-century pubs were swept away in the 1950s and '60s but some, like the Wheatsheaf, were rebuilt as modern pubs. *(NW)*

The Woodsman, Dudley Wood, May 1992. *(Jeff Parkes)*

The Bunch of Bluebells on the corner of Crabourne Road and Saltwells Road was opened in the spring of 1957, serving the large postwar Saltwells estates, and is seen in 1992. This pub and the Moot Meet on Halesowen Road were both new Ansell's pubs opened during that year. In the 1900s this had been the site of Jacky Dunn's Pool among the wastes of the long worked-out Saltwells Collieries. *(Jeff Parkes)*

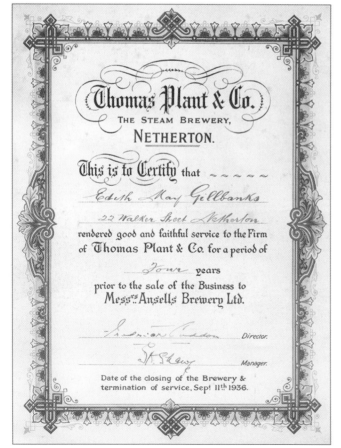

Plant's Steam Brewery was on the corner of St John's Street and Halesowen Road, right behind the Castle pub. The site was cleared in the 1960s and the Mash Tun was built on it but this has now been demolished and modern flats occupy the site. *Above:* A Plant's Brewery staff outing – probably a 'breakfast club' with Holdens Coaches, whose drivers are on the right. Only William Stevens, fourth from left on the front row, has been identified. *(Dorothy Rollason)*

This 1938 long-service certificate marks the closure of the brewery, Ansell's having taken it over in 1936. *(Dave Whyley)*

7
Netherton in the Classroom

The first schools provided in Netherton were established by the Church of England and were known as National Schools. Legend has it that some funds were left over from building St Andrew's Church and these were used to build a school.

It was built at the junction with the Halesowen Road and the new road built up to the church – Church Road – and this opened in 1836. The school was in fact two schools, one for boys and one for girls, separated by the headmaster's house. Church schools were eventually established at Darby End (1871) and Dudley Wood alongside mission churches. The church also opened St Andrew's Infants School, Hill Street, in 1873.

The 1870 Education Act established School Boards, and the Dudley School Board covered Netherton. At first the board rented Sunday School rooms and opened its first board school in Brewery Street in 1877. The Iron Schools in Halesowen Road followed in 1885 and the Northfield Road School in 1891.

A postcard view of the Church of England School at the junction of Church Road and Halesowen Road, *c.* 1905. The headmaster's house in the centre of the building can be seen clearly. The school closed in 1907 as the building was being undermined by subsidence and it was demolished immediately. The foundation stone for its replacement was laid on 30 December 1907 (St Andrew's Day). *(Ken Rock)*

The Brewery Street School of 1877 in Cinder Bank was not an elegant building compared to some built by the school board, and looked the worse for wear when awaiting demolition one hundred years later. The site is now occupied by an older persons' residential home. *(NHG)*

Class V at the Brewery Street School, 1931. Please smile for the camera! *(W. Boyd)*

The Dudley School Board purchased land from the Earl of Dudley in 1889 and H. Dorse & Son of Cradley Heath set about building a school designed by Messrs Pincher & Long of West Bromwich. It was opened on 10 January 1891 by the Chairman of the Board, Alderman Billing, to accommodate 200 girls and 256 mixed infants. *(NW)*

A new Infants' School was opened on an adjacent site on 29 September 1913 and the former Girls' Department became a Senior Mixed School for some time. The buildings are now exclusively in primary school use. *(NW)*

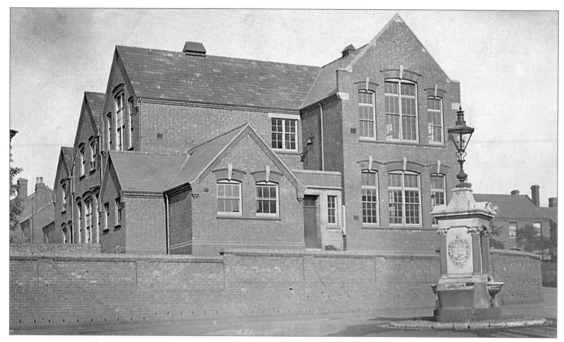

The replacement for the old 1836 church school was this large two-storey building erected by W.H. Deeley and designed by F.W. Glazebrook. It was opened on 24 February 1908. The two floors enabled boys and girls to be educated separately but after 1931 the lower part of the school became 'Mixed Juniors' and the upper part became 'Mixed Seniors' – bearing in mind that the school leaving age was then 14. For a short while after 1972 it was used as a middle school but it closed in the mid-1980s and since 1989 it has been in retail use. Note the drinking fountain at Cradley Road junction; this was later moved to the park. *(Ken Rock)*

The Iron Schools (Halesowen Road) – awaiting demolition in 1962. They had opened on 14 March 1885. *(Jeff Parkes)*

The staff at the Halesowen Road Iron Schools in 1953. The only teachers identified are Mr Horridge, the headmaster, in the centre; Mr Billingham, 2nd from right in the front row, Miss Baker, 3rd from right in the front row, and Mr Stewart, 3rd from right in the back row. *(NHG)*

Boys from the Halesowen Road Secondary School (the Iron Schools), attending the annual camp at Astley Burgh in June 1956. On the left stands Mr Hallam and on the right Mr Stewart. *(NHG)*

Above: Miss Dunn and a successful girls' team from the Halesowen Road Secondary School, *c.* 1960. *Below:* a winning boys' team of 1955. *(NHG)*

Halesowen Rd. Sec. Sch.
Winners
Manchester United Cub
1955

When the Halesowen Road Secondary School had to leave the old Iron Schools building it moved to this new block: Saltwells Secondary Modern School, opened in September 1962. Ultimately the school was amalgamated with Hillcrest School, and the building has now become Dudley's Educational Development Unit. *(NW)*

Learning new sports at Saltwells Secondary: the School Archery Team in 1964. Mr Harthill (left) and Mr Nottingham (right) with, left to right: Carl Price, Michael Kendrick, Ivan Johnson, Phillip Fleet, Geoff Whitehouse and Barry Gulbridge. *(NHG)*

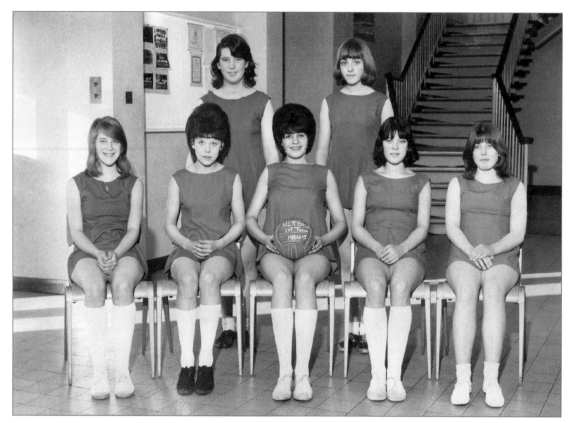

1964/5 school teams pose in the main corridor and stairwell of Saltwells Secondary School: the Netball Team (above), and the Football Team. *(NHG)*

Recipients of Duke of Edinburgh Awards at Saltwells Secondary School in November 1975. Only the names of Anthony Blair and Adrian White have been recorded for posterity. *(NHG)*

Children at the short-lived Saltwells First School celebrate the Queen's Silver Jubilee in 1977 with a party. The Aldi supermarket is now on this site. *(Ann Harris)*

Hillcrest School and Community College as it is today. It was opened on 10 January 1958 by
Sir Edward Thompson, as Hillcrest Secondary School. It was the first of its type in the Borough
of Dudley and had cost £110,000. It was designed by John Lewis, the Borough Architect, and
built by J. Hickman of Brierley Hill. Two hundred and fifty pupils from Northfield Road School
were its first pupils. The idea of giving the school a Community College role came at the end of
the 1970s. (NW)

Netherbrook Primary School began life as Bowling Green Junior School when opened by
George Wigg MP on 26 March 1954. It was reopened as Netherbrook Primary School in
1984, its name referring to Netherton's nearby Mousesweet Brook. (NW)

The Church of England had first established a school at Dudley Wood using the wooden building that became St Barnabas' Mission. These buildings, seen here in 2005, were opened on 15 April 1931 by the Mayor of Dudley, Alderman John Molyneux, who was also President of Dudley Co-operative Society. It was regarded as an innovative 'open-air' school for 200 children, consisting of four classrooms which could be opened to the elements. It had cost £8,800 to build, much of which had to be spent on stabilising the ground. It was designed by Messrs Scott & Clark of Wednesbury. One of the four original teachers, Vera Whorton (née Woodward), returned to the school in April 1981 to celebrate the school's Golden Jubilee. *(NW)*

Boys and girls share double desks and pose for the camera in the bright modern airy classrooms of Dudley Wood Junior School, 1936. These wooden desks on iron frames lasted until the 1960s. Books are ready and open – but visual aids seem a bit sparse. *(Jeff Parkes Collection)*

Children at Dudley Wood Junior School prepare to celebrate the coronation of Elizabeth II, 2 June 1953. *(Jeff Parkes Collection)*

Alison Parkes crowns her classmate Anne Raybould as May Queen at Dudley Wood Junior School, summer 1959. *(Jeff Parkes Collection)*

Children at play at Yew Tree Primary School. A modern school built on land between the Cricket Club's ground and St Andrew's churchyard, it opened on 25 March 1953 (see p. 26). Between 1974 and 1989 it was known as Yew Tree First School. When the school at the foot of Church Road closed in 1989 Yew Tree became Netherton Church of England Primary School. *(NHG)*

Children at Yew Tree Junior School in the 1950s take part in the annual Nativity Play. Maureen Smith played the Virgin Mary, but the names of the others are not recorded. *(Shirley Lynall Collection)*

Children at Yew Tree Primary School presenting *Snow White and the Seven Dwarfs* as their Christmas play, 1975. *(Joan White Collection)*

May queens and plays about dwarfs may no longer be politically correct but back in 1955 no one seemed worried about crowning Angela Aston as May Queen at Yew Tree Primary School. *(Joan White Collection)*

Joan White, left, and Linda Button, right, pose with pupils at Yew Tree Primary School for a standard class photograph in 1986. *(Joan White Collection)*

Staff at Yew Tree Primary School pose for the photographer in the late 1970s. Back row: left to right, Hazel Province, Josie Dunn, -?-, Elisabeth Brierley, -?-, Linda Button. Front row: Dorothy Andrews (welfare), Nora Underhill (secretary), Joan White (headteacher), Cynthia Nunn, Cath Davies. *(Joan White Collection)*

Yew Tree Primary School, now Netherton C of E Primary School, faces the busy Highbridge Road, now used by traffic to and from Merry Hill. Here we see crossing patrol lady Maureen Hackett coping with traffic and children at the end of the 1980s. *(Joan White Collection)*

During the 1970s when coal was open-cast mined from Netherton Hill, the banks came very close to Yew Tree Primary School. This picture is taken from the top of the mound towering over the school. Beyond the school is the caretaker's house, the vicarage and tower blocks in Netherton. *(Joan White Collection)*

8
Church & Chapel

Did churches and chapels outnumber pubs in Netherton? Or was it the other way round? Having become a Church of England parish in the first half of the nineteenth century, it eventually subdivided and the missions to Dudley Wood and Darby End were elevated to parish status.

Chapels have been numerous, starting with a very early congregation giving its name to a part of Netherton: Baptist End. The dissenters who eventually formed the Congregationalists of King Street, Dudley, felt it was their duty to promote their faith in poorer and less civilised districts. They helped establish the chapel in Primrose Hill. Methodists came in all shapes and sizes. The Wesleyans, New Connexion and Primitive Methodists all established themselves in Netherton, while further groups of Baptists had built chapels at Sweet Turf and Ebenezer. The latter congregation took their faith to the Lodge Farm Estate and built a chapel there.

The Black Country love of independence nourished other groups who built the People's Mission Hall in Swan Street, the Emmanuel Church in Sledmere, and the Wesley Bible Institute in Darby End. The Christadelphians also have long had a presence in Netherton.

St Andrew's Church – concealed behind trees and enjoying a remote position on top of a hill. This Reeves postcard of Church Road captures the location of the church well. The vicarage is hidden on the left. The walls on the right still stand. (*Trudi Blair*)

St Andrew's Church, surrounded by trees and its hilltop churchyard, can only be photographed effectively during the winter. The foundation stone was laid on 30 November 1827, and on 16 July 1830 people marched from St Thomas's at Dudley to open the new church, at that time just a chapel-at-ease to St Thomas's. It was built at a cost of £8,000 and accommodated 1,500 people. Netherton became a separate parish on 1 December 1844. *(NW)*

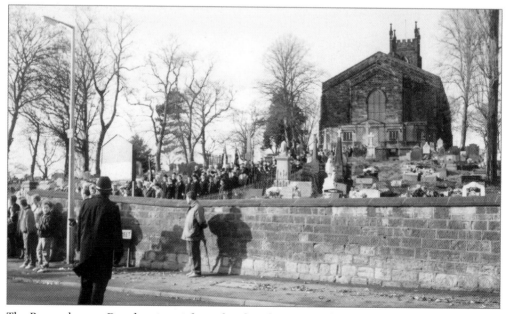

The Remembrance Parade sets out from the church in November 1992, although it was more usual for the parade to assemble at Northfield Road and march to the church. Some trees in front of the church were destroyed by Dutch Elm disease. *(NHG)*

The fabric and interior of St Andrew's has been enhanced by many gifts over the years plus several restorations. The organ was installed in 1835; bells were donated in 1861 and again in 1897. The ornamental iron screen was erected in 1892 and combined the work of N. Hingley & Sons and other local craftsmen. The east window was donated by Blanche Skidmore. A new pulpit was added in 1903, donated by G.H. Dunn, a key figure in the political development of Netherton within Dudley. (*W. Boyd*)

Canon Stevens (vicar 1947–79) and the church choir at St Andrew's, *c.* 1970. (*Joyce Holden*)

A large vicarage was provided at St Andrew's on ground well below the level of the top of Church Road – a site now occupied by the modern houses of Alpine Drive. The vicarage itself has been replaced with a modern house in Highbridge Road. *(Reeves postcard: Trudi Blair)*

St Andrew's Church Choir heading for St Thomas's Church, Dudley, June 1948. The Co-op is on the left. *(Joyce Holden)*

The Bishop of Worcester and (right) the Revd Billy Barnes, vicar of Netherton, dedicate a St George's flag on the altar at St Andrew's on St George's Day, 23 April 2005. The flag was then flown from the church tower in July to celebrate the 175th birthday of St Andrew's Church. *(NW)*

The predominantly red banner of the Sunday School, and the predominantly blue banner of the Mothers' Union at St Andrew's, Netherton. *(NW)*

St Andrew's Church Choir assembles in the old Market Place in 1953 to lead a procession back to the church. In the centre of the crowd is Len Homer, the Netherton postmaster. *(Harry Rose)*

Everyone in their Sunday best: the St Andrew's Church procession of 1953 passes the New Inns and Raybould's Fold as it makes its way along High Street. *(Harry Rose)*

Just as St Andrew's hides behind its trees, St Peter's hides below the level of the road! The church began life in 1871 as a National School for the children of Darby End, using a building which later became the church hall. Sunday School and Sunday evening services were also provided. When the Iron Schools opened in 1885 it became a mission church, usually looked after by curates from St Andrew's. In 1910 Father Wareham arrived as Priest in Charge, introducing a High Church style and the plans to build a more permanent church. This building was opened on 11 January 1913. The former church building continued to be used as the Church Hall until it was replaced in 1957. St Peter's acquired parish church status in 1977. *(NW)*

St Peter's Sunday School Anniversary procession in 1911 shown in a Fred Perkins (of Netherton) postcard. With the Wesleyan Chapel behind them the children begin to make their way back up Northfield Road. *(Ken Rock)*

Father Thompson arrived at St Peter's in 1937: these two photographs were taken during his residency. He takes part in the 1941 Anniversary Parade on Bumble Hole Road. *(Doris Corbett Collection)*

Father Thompson, on the right, pauses just outside the door to St Peter's Church one Sunday just after the Second World War. The group consists of Sunday School teachers: left to right: Joan Willetts, Joyce Alliband, Mrs Kinnerley, Mrs Willetts Snr, Joe Bissell, Ronnie Willetts, Doris Corbett (almost hidden), Brenda Cooper, Rex Gadd and Arthur Harris. *(Doris Corbett Collection)*

St Peter's Church Choir takes to the pavement outside the church entrance, *c.* 1952. There is a rare glimpse of the old church hall on the extreme left. Canon Stevens is in the centre. *(Doris Corbett)*

The interior of St Peter's Church, which in more recent years has been made less cluttered, but the chairs have been retained. *(Doris Corbett)*

Canon Stevens from St Andrew's and Father Peacock from St Peter's take part in the St Peter's Sunday School Anniversary Parade in about 1972, passing modern houses in what has become St Peter's Road. *(Rita Darby)*

St Peter's Church Mothers' Union holds a cake sale on the forecourt of the church hall as part of a coffee morning, early 1990s. These ladies are Beatrice Willetts, Nellie Betteridge, Joy Fellows, Kath Faulkner, Dorothy Summerfield, Joyce Spencer and Iris Alliband. *(Doris Corbett Collection)*

Bishop Tony Dumper of
Dudley with Father Lambert,
who came to St Peter's in
1976, to become its first vicar
the following year. *(Doris
Corbett Collection)*

Processing round St Peter's
Church on Consecration Day
in 1977, showing the church's
proximity to the canal. Rita
Darby and Ann Harris are on
the left, followed by Jack
Darby, Sam Brookes, Peter
Harris, Bill Foster, Philip
Alliband and others.
(Iris Alliband Collection)

The Church of England also opened a National School in Dudley Wood, operating in the same way as St Peter's in Darby End: day school from Monday to Friday, and religious use on Sunday. It was a second-hand wooden building and was given the name of St Barnabas. When its brick replacement was built it remained in use as a Sunday School until 1954. This picture was taken in about 1905 and is the only known picture to show the exterior of St Barnabas. *(Keith Hodgkins)*

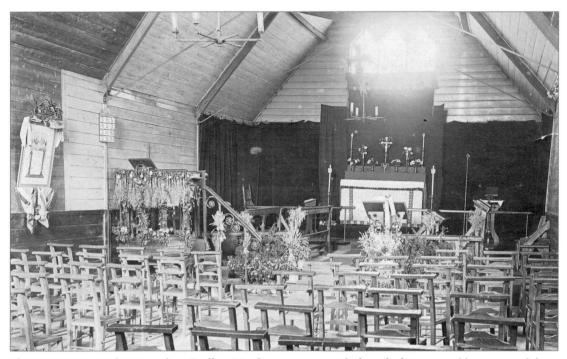

This interior view of St Barnabas, Dudley Wood, gives us a good idea of what it was like in one of these simple wooden structures. The chairs seem to be of the same pattern as those at St Peter's. *(NHG)*

The Men's Bible Class at St Barnabas' Mission in about 1905 gives us another tantalising glimpse of the wooden building. *(Olwen Chilton)*

The Mothers' Union Banner at St John's was given by the Nicklin family and features the Virgin Mary under a tree. The bell and keys – all that remain of the original St Barnabas – are kept on display at St John's. *(NW)*

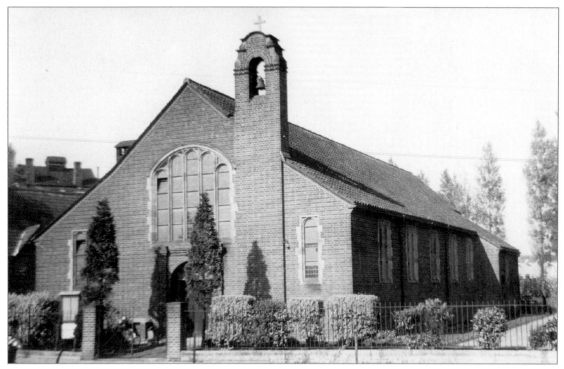

On 1 October 1912 Mrs Abigail Hampton died and bequeathed £19,000 to the incumbent of St Andrew's so that he might build a brick replacement for the little wooden mission church at Dudley Wood. One condition was that the new church be dedicated to St John. St John's was designed by Sir Charles Nicholson and was opened and consecrated on 30 October 1930. On 29 September 1949 St John's was reconsecrated as a parish church, separating itself from St Andrew's. The attractive little church is built right on the boundary of Netherton as the Mousesweet Brook runs alongside the car park. *Below:* The interior when new. *(Both pictures Olwen Chilton)*

Above: The choir, with the vicar, the Revd Ron Crisp, in the centre, assembles outside the church hall at St John's, Dudley Wood, on 9 June 1964. The building was designed by Stanley Griffiths and built by J.M. Tate of Cradley in 1954. (Stanley Griffiths came along and carved the eagle in wet cement on the front of the building.) *Below:* Shortly after the above photograph was taken, the choir was leading the Sunday School Anniversary Parade around Dudley Wood. *(Olwen Chilton)*

St John's Church Choir, Dudley Wood, in the 1940s. Back row, left to right: Ben Green, Arthur Tromans, Sam Johnson, Joe Billingham (later Mayor of Dudley – see p. 149), Horace Wycherley, Bill Boxley, Mr Frost, Tom Bradbury, Eris Bishop and Joseph Griffiths – of the Mushroom Green chain manufacturers. Middle row: Jennie Guest, Jean Westwood, Laura Billingham, Revd Owen, Queenie Lloyd, Madge Nicholls and Christine Billingham. The lads in the front row have not been identified. Beyond the trees there were allotments but in recent years housing has spread across this area. *(Brian Grundy)*

The St John's Sunday School Anniversary Parade of 1965 is seen passing Dudley Wood Primary School in Dudley Wood Road on its way back to the church. *(Brian Grundy)*

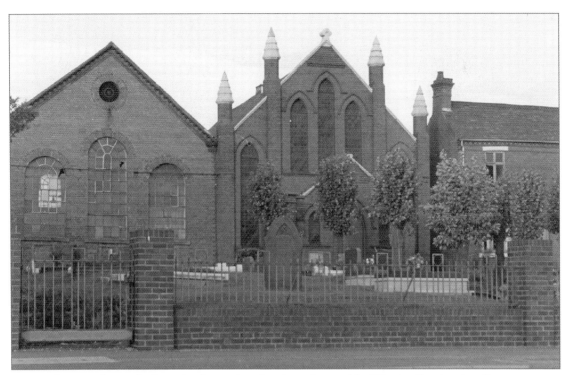

Moving from Netherton's three Anglican churches into the world of Nonconformists, we first encounter the Baptists. This picture was taken of Messiah Chapel, Cinder Bank, on 7 October 1979 on the occasion of the Harvest Festival and the final service to be held there. Baptists have been around in Netherton since 1654 and built their first chapel in the area, which became known as Baptist End. They came to Cinder Bank in 1746, and this particular building was erected in 1831. The burial ground in the foreground still survives, but the chapel was demolished after the last service. *(Brian Roberts)*

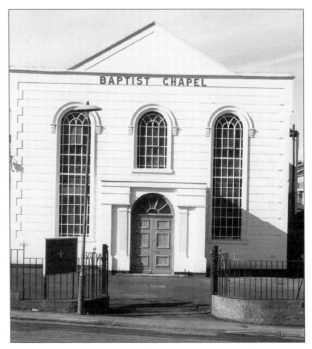

The Particular Baptists at Sweet Turf Chapel trace their history back to a congregation of thirteen that formed in 1810, and were more 'Calvinistic' than the folks at Messiah. It is not clear how soon after 1810 they were able to build this chapel, which took its name from the well-watered meadow between Cinder Bank and Simms Lane. The elegant frontage of the chapel has been modified by a modern extension and the church is now used by the Champions Church: an independent evangelical group. *(NHG)*

The Sunday School Anniversary at Sweet Turf Chapel, June 1964. In the centre of the picture is A.J. Wilkinson, who had left Sweet Turf to establish the mission at Lodge Farm. (He owned a well-known tailor's shop in Netherton High Street.) To the left of Mr Wilkinson is his brother-in-law, John Horace Bill, the organist, and to his right is his daughter, Audrey Wilkinson, who trained the children for the anniversary. *(Ruth Pugh)*

A group of Baptists at Sweet Turf broke away in 1864 to form a General Baptist congregation. They quickly set about building their own chapel in St Andrew's Road, and the building seen here in 2004 was completed early in 1865. It took the name 'Ebenezer', a popular name with the General Baptists, and in 1875 added a schoolroom at the back of this building. *(NW)*

From the 1960s onwards the Ebenezer Chapel faced decline, but more recently it has revived and this 2004 picture of the interior shows that a great deal of refurbishment has taken place. At one time the ceiling had sunk on to the top of the organ pipes, and one of the tasks undertaken recently was to push the ceiling back to its original place! *(NW)*

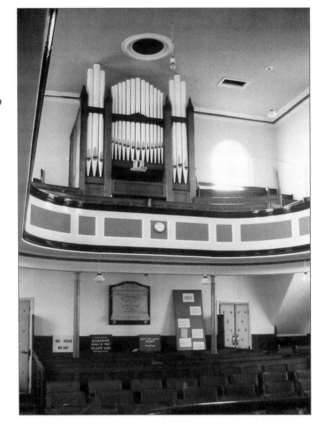

When the Lodge Farm Estate was being built in 1949, A.J. Wilkinson and some other Baptists from Sweet Turf decided to provide a Sunday School in a builder's hut. On 11 March 1950 they opened their purpose-built hall. *(Madge & Ray Cole)*

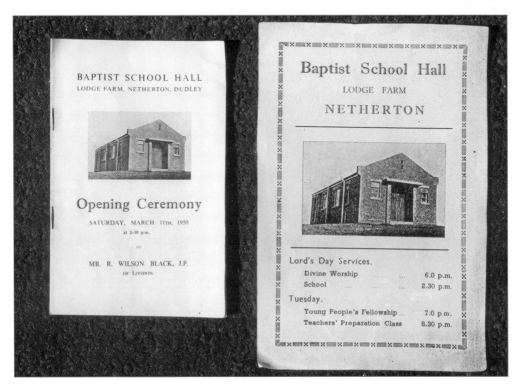

Above: The modest interior of Lodge Farm Chapel, seen in 2004, from which the congregation has striven to serve the community. *(NW)*

Left: the Wednesday Afternoon Ladies' Class, 1950s. *(Madge & Ray Cole)*

Below: The Boys' Brigade parade around the estate from the chapel in the early 1950s, when some of the original prefabs could still be seen. *(Madge & Ray Cole)*

Madge and Ray Cole set up successful companies of the Boys' Brigade and the Girls' Brigade based at the chapel on Lodge Farm. Ray Cole (top right) and the 2nd Dudley Company of the Boys' Brigade, 1977.

Madge Cole (top right) and the 2nd Netherton Company of the Girls' Brigade at Lodge Farm, 1977. (*Both pictures Ray & Madge Cole Collection*)

When the Congregationalists in Dudley (King Street) decided to support the spread of their denomination to Netherton it seems that they deliberately targeted the working-class industrialised quarter of Primrose Hill rather than the growing commercial centre of the township. John Fraser Watkins (1812–1900) organised cottage-based worship in the area until they were ready to build a chapel. The foundation stone of the first building was laid on 8 May 1871 and it was opened the following February. By the mid-1880s subsidence was having its effect, and a replacement chapel was opened on 28 November 1887, but by 1911 even this building was on the verge of collapse. After the First World War work began on rebuilding the chancel after laying another foundation stone on 15 December 1919. The chapel reopened in July 1920 – as seen here – only to have to rebuild the Sunday School building in about 1932. (*Joe Guest*)

A faded picture used in a 1910 Netherton Sunday Schools booklet to remind people of the fate of the first Primrose Hill Chapel. By the mid-1880s subsidence had almost wrecked the building. (*Albert Willetts Collection*)

Pictures of the fabric of Primrose Hill Chapel inevitably tend to show it collapsing or being rebuilt! Here we see the old chancel end wall awaiting demolition at the time of the First World War. Fortunately it was possible to rebuild it while retaining the central window although it had to be raised above a new porch (see opposite page). *(Joe Guest)*

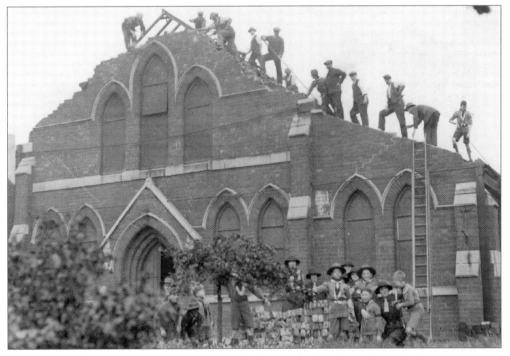

The Sunday School building, glimpsed behind the trees in the top picture on the opposite page, collapsed at the end of the 1920s, and here we see volunteers, assisted by the Scouts, demolishing the building. It was replaced by 1932. *(Joe Guest)*

If they are not demolishing or rebuilding their chapel, the folks at Primrose Hill are cleaning or refurbishing it. *Above:* The Sunday School Rebuilding Group of *c.* 1930: 5th and 6th from left, back row, are the minister, Walter Parry, and by his side William Shaw, the Chapel Secretary. In the front row on the left is Ernest Bill, a steeplejack from Hingley's who helped rebuild the Sunday School and lived to be 101. *(Joe Guest)*

Left: Refurbishing and cleaning the chapel in 1987, assisted by the Community Programme. Left to right, back: Mrs Ball, Mrs Mackintosh and Mrs Turley; front: Alma Guest, Brian Turley, Lily Yardley. *(Joe Guest)*

There has always been a close tie between Primrose Hill and Messrs Hingley's Ironworks, where many of the congregation worked. In recent times the war memorial from Hingley's was moved from the abandoned factory to Primrose Hill Chapel. The Mayor of Dudley, Councillor Sam Davies, who unveiled the memorial in 1989, is flanked by Canon Fred Wilcox of St Andrew's, on the right, and Joe Guest of Primrose Hill.

Primrose Hill Chapel elders and deacons, 1990s. Back row, left to right: Mervyn Willetts (secretary), Albert Butler, Ivor Lucas (treasurer), Joe Guest. Front row: George Biggins, Fred Lavender, Andy Kevern, Susan Williams, Janice Cole, Susan Ball. *(Both pictures Joe Guest)*

As we move on to look at the Methodists in Netherton it is usual to begin with the Wesleyans. In many towns the Wesleyan Methodists were tradespeople who could afford a reasonable chapel fairly close to the town centre. In the case of Netherton a Wesleyan Society that was in existence by 1810 seemed to be filled with miners from Darby End. In 1820 they acquired land and on 1 April 1821 they opened their chapel at Cole Street, in the centre of Darby End. Like so many others it was affected by subsidence and had to be rebuilt. It reopened in this form on 29 February 1904. *(Albert Willetts)*

The 1904 rebuild of the 1821 building at Cole Street was in need of further rebuilding by 1938 when a fund was launched for that purpose. The Second World War intervened and the final service in the old chapel did not take place until 14 May 1950. Services were then held in the Sunday School. The brand new chapel seen here was opened on 3 October 1959. *(Bert Beard Collection)*

The interior of the 1959 building at Cole Street when new: a forerunner of 1960s chapel design. In this picture the chairs are facing the altar and pulpit. The hall was designed so that the chairs could be turned round to face a stage at the other end. *(Bert Beard Collection)*

The stage end of the chapel can be fully exploited during Sunday School anniversaries and here we see members of the choir and Sunday School presenting excerpts from *Joseph and the Amazing Technicolor Dreamcoat* in their anniversary service of 20 June 2004. *(NW)*

In the mid-1860s it seems that a dozen Wesleyans from Cole Street decided they should establish a congregation that could meet in the centre of Netherton, knowing that the New Connexion Methodists had done so since 1848, and the Prims since 1851. After using Mr Downing's bakehouse in Cradley Road, they acquired land in Church Street. In 1865 they open a small chapel/Sunday School at the rear of this site. While looking forward to the day when they could build a bigger chapel fronting Church Road, the 1865 building was wrecked by subsidence. In 1893 they acquired a 'tin tabernacle' from Trinity Congregational Chapel in Birmingham and we see it here 'rebuilt' in Church Street. *(Cyril Wright)*

In 1912 the tin tabernacle was sold (to become a cinema in Gornal Wood) and construction of its brick successor began. Here we see the new building as it was when opened on 6 January 1913. Looking at the side of the chapel reveals the brick foundations on which the tin chapel had stood – and which now became a cellar to the 1913 building. The name Trinity was not adopted until 1991 when the congregation was joined by the folks from St John's. *(Cyril Wright)*

The large organ at the Church Road Wesleyan Chapel was added in March 1914, completing the warm interior of the building. The text above the arch has been painted over in subsequent redecorations, but otherwise the interior remains little changed. *(Cyril Wright)*

As already stated, the New Connexion Methodists were quick off the mark in Netherton. Their first society was established by 1819 and in 1827 they opened a chapel at Eagle Hill. They quickly outgrew this and built the chapel seen here in St John's Street – with a front that had been rebuilt in 1898. Was the street named after the chapel, or was it the other way round? St John's survived to become one of six chapels forming a Netherton Methodist circuit in 1966, but closed its doors on 31 December 1990 when it amalgamated with Church Road to form 'Trinity'. An independent Pentecostal congregation now uses it. *(Muriel Woodhouse)*

The interior of St John's Chapel, St John's Street, not to be confused with St John's, Dudley Wood, photographed in the 1980s when the new Pentecostal congregation had started restoration work on the fabric of the building. *(NHG)*

The New Connexion Methodists were also active at Darby End. This chapel, photographed in about 1910, and known as 'Providence', was opened on Northfield Road on 29 January 1837 and played a very active part in the history of Darby End, along with Cole Street and St Peter's. The final service was held at Providence on 25 August 1974, after which the caretaker contacted the Black Country Museum to see if they would be interested in saving any items. The museum said they were interested in the whole chapel! Providence was rededicated in its new home at the Black Country Living Museum on 15 September 1979. The whole Providence story is retold in *From Alpha to Omega*, published in 2004 to mark its 25th anniversary in the museum. *(Albert Willetts Collection)*

The Primitive Methodists began meeting in the Primrose Hill area of Netherton in the 1840s. They purchased land in Cradley Road in about 1850 and opened their first chapel, known as Noah's Ark, in 1851, adding a substantial Sunday School building in 1898. Subsidence caused by mining attacked the first building in common with most other Netherton chapels, and in 1924 a fund was launched to build a replacement. On 16 March 1925 the stone-laying ceremony for the new chapel took place – as seen here – in front of the 1898 building. *(Chapel Collection)*

The new Noah's Ark was opened and dedicated on 23 November 1925, built at a cost of £4,455. It is shown here in a Reeves' postcard of the 1930s. *(Trudi Blair)*

Sunday School teachers at Noah's Ark, *c.* 1910. The Primitive Methodists had established a Dudley Circuit of four chapels: George Street, replaced by Vicar Street, Dudley, Wellington Road, Dudley, Woodside and Noah's Ark at Netherton. (Later Tipton Street, Sedgley, was added.). Noah's Ark was remarkable for the range of its activities: Band of Hope, Women's Guild, Bible Study groups, Drama Society, Boys' Brigade, Youth Club and the Anti-Cigarette League! *(Chapel Collection)*

A Sunday School banner survived at Noah's Ark until closure. It is being displayed here by Rita and Graham Faulkner, Brian Handy and David Willetts, in March 2004, in front of the 1898 Sunday School building, which still stands today. *(NW)*

In the mid-1890s a group of Baptists from Messiah Chapel broke away to form an independent congregation. They rented a field in Swan Street and in just six weeks in 1898 they erected a tin tabernacle from a kit and opened as the People's Mission Hall. The official opening was on 28 September 1898 and the membership at the time was twenty-six. This photograph was taken in 1910 for the Netherton Sunday School Festival of that year. *(Albert Willetts Collection)*

The People's Mission outgrew its tin tabernacle and on 22 July 1932 the foundation stone was laid for this brick building. The iron building survived in Sunday School use until a new one was opened on 6 October 1961. *(NW)*

The Swan Street People's Mission Hall was famous for its choirs and Sunday School, and here we see a modern Sunday School anniversary taking place on 13 June 2004 beneath the magnificent banner, led by Brian Payton (in front of the organ). Above the banner can be seen the legend: 'Enter His Courts with Praise' which became the title of a history of the mission published to mark its 1998 centenary. *(NW)*

The People's Mission Hall Sunday School Anniversary Parade sets out along Swan Street, in 1949. (Another picture of this parade appears on p. 27.) *(Harry Rose)*

The People's Mission Hall held open-air meetings in Windmill End; the Darby End New Connexion held meetings at Springfield that led to building the chapel at Knowle. Here, in 1957, we see the tradition of the open air, or 'tent meeting', continuing as Arthur Parkes and Ben Bird, from Swan Street, engaged the evangelist Adam Cambers to lead a crusade on the new Sledmere Estate. The crowd includes the Revd T.H. Evans, later a minister, and Trevor Lowe, who is present leader of Emmanuel Church, Sledmere. *(Trevor Lowe)*

From the tent meetings at Sledmere a congregation was formed and in 1959 we see a group proudly standing outside their new Emmanuel Church. Left to right: Ben Bird, Michael Parkes, Mrs Bird, Nancy Parkes, Betty Hill, Wendy Saunders. Front row: Jeremy Parkes and Jane Bird (now Lowe). *(Trevor Lowe)*

The Emmanuel Church, St George's Road, Sledmere, seen here in 2005. It was designed by Norman Trickett and built by John Whitehouse, although the original intention was to provide a bigger building, or possibly expand to the rear of this building. Like all institutions it has had its ups and downs over the years but has raised thousands of pounds for missionary work, and many Sunday School children have passed through its doors. *(NW)*

The congregation at Emmanuel Church, Sledmere, fit very snugly into this compact building. They are currently led by Trevor Lowe, son-in-law of one of the founders, Ben Bird. Although this interior was badly damaged by a fire in 2005, it has been refurbished and opened again in January 2006. *(NW)*

In 1914 some ground alongside Cole Street, Darby End, was purchased by Dan Morby with the intention of building the 'Young People's Christian Institute'. It seems that this was a break-away group from the Cole Street Wesleyan Chapel, but, as can be seen from the picture, they were very much in the independent 'Let's-build-it-ourselves' mould. Foundation stones were laid on 12 June 1915 and the building was probably completed later that year. *(Betty Nash)*

The Wesley Bible Institute, Cole Street, still alive and well in 2005. The congregation did much to keep young men occupied during periods of unemployment and built up a very successful football team (see p. 10). In 1931 an extra commemorative stone was laid alongside the 1915 foundation stones in memory of Joseph Darby. *(NW)*

A Sunday School Anniversary at the Wesley Bible Institute, *c.* 1935. *(Betty Nash)*

The institute's magnificent George Tuthill banner. *(Betty Nash)*

Methodists at Dudley Wood assemble for the opening of their new chapel in Dudley Wood Road on 23 October 1907. This replaced an earlier building which had been affected by subsidence and had been built by Methodists based in Mushroom Green.

Miss Olwen Bytheway and the Revd Arthur Page watch an 1866 Sunday School foundation stone being re-laid for the new school in 1960. *(Both pictures Fred & Winnie Emery Collection)*

The old 1866 wooden Sunday School buildings at Dudley Wood Methodist Chapel, on the right, were about to be demolished in 1959, and the crowd here takes part in an event to raise funds for its replacement.

The interior of the Dudley Wood Methodist Chapel. *(Both pictures Jeff Parkes)*

On 26 May 1957 the Mayor of Dudley's Civic Service was held at Dudley Wood Methodist Chapel because the new mayor, Councillor Joe Billingham, was a Dudley Wood lad. Here he is seen leading the civic procession along Dudley Wood Road with the Town Clerk, Mr Wadsworth, and the Mayor's Chaplain, the Revd D.H. Swanbury. *(Jeff Parkes)*

The last service was held in Dudley Wood Methodist Church on 8 May 2005, taking the form of a Sunday School Anniversary. The congregation, pictured here at an earlier service, then moved to classrooms behind the hall in the Sunday School building, while alterations were made to that facility. The chapel was sold to a developer and it has since been demolished to make way for housing. *(NW)*

The Christadelphians had become established in Netherton at the end of the nineteenth century, first meeting in each other's homes. Eventually they were able to buy this building in St Thomas Street, an ex-Scout building, and meetings were held there until 1972.

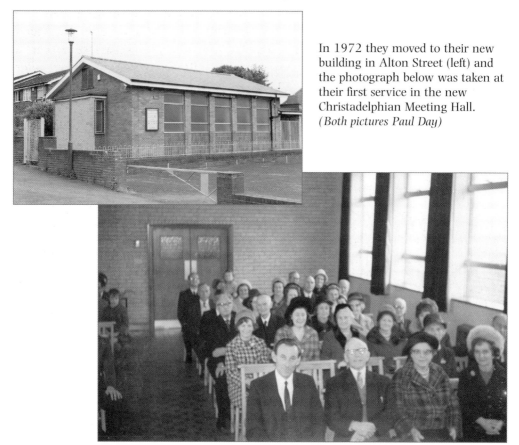

In 1972 they moved to their new building in Alton Street (left) and the photograph below was taken at their first service in the new Christadelphian Meeting Hall. *(Both pictures Paul Day)*

9

Having Fun in Netherton

There was more to Netherton than digging for coal or making chains. Nethertonians worked hard but they also led very full lives. There was no lack of social and cultural activities in which to engage. As has already been seen, much of this may have revolved around pubs or the world of church and chapel.

Old photographs portray Nethertonians participating in sporting activities, drama groups, choirs, Scouts, Guides and Boys' Brigade, friendly societies, Toc H, Sons of Rest, St John Ambulance Brigade, among others.

Netherton had two cinemas, one effectively replacing the other, and it had a public hall and library, which graduated into the Netherton Art Centre. There was abundant open space, ranging from the park, to the fields around the rezzer (reservoir), Saltwells Woods, and the Yew Tree Hills, and canal towpaths to explore. In the 1960s, after a week's work you could have attended a WEA evening class or choir practice on Friday evening. All your Saturday morning shopping could be completed in Netherton, you could go water skiing in the afternoon and watch *Hamlet* at the Art Centre in the evening. The next day you could take part in a Sunday School Anniversary and walk round the Rezzer in the afternoon, after sampling some real ale at the Old Swan.

Although the date on the drum is '1906' it has not been possible to find out much about the Netherton Colliery Band. The colliery consisted of pits in the Baptist End area and was virtually worked out by 1900 when land was about to be levelled to create a recreation ground. *(Ken Rock)*

The hall decorated for the coronation of Elizabeth II in 1953. *(Harry Rose)*

After Dudley Council had opened its own Central Library, attention was turned to Woodside and Netherton. A temporary reading room was provided in September 1884 and a library was opened on 17 February 1885. Meanwhile, the Earl of Dudley was persuaded to make land available for something more permanent. On 5 July 1893 the Countess of Dudley laid the foundation stone of the building seen above. It was designed by Tom Grazebrook and built by Messrs Willetts of Old Hill. It was paid for with funds raised at Dudley's Castle Fêtes. On 24 July 1894 the Netherton Public Hall, or 'Institute' was opened, with library and reading room included. (Woodside had parallel treatment.) It immediately became the focus of the cultural life of Netherton. The £6,000 project included a fire station and three police houses, two cells and a 'shed' for tramps.

On 1 January 1910 Howard Bishop obtained a licence to show films in the main hall – at first on an occasional basis, and then, from November 1910, on a more regular basis. After 1932 the lease was only renewed for a year at a time and by the end of the 1930s film shows were abandoned. As a cinema it was always known to Nethertonians as 'Bungies' or 'The Stute'.

After the war the hall was redeveloped in a pioneering joint venture between Dudley Corporation and the Arts Council of Great Britain. It reopened as the Netherton Art Centre on 29 August 1947 with a Midland Theatre Company production of *Frieda*. This company regularly put on plays (one week in three) until the opening of the Belgrade Theatre in Coventry. The gap was then filled by Dudley Little Theatre.

Netherton Park was a similar venture. In 1900 Dudley Corporation borrowed the unheard-of sum of £18,000 to create recreation grounds at Woodside and Netherton, on areas that had been colliery waste. Parks and public halls were symbols of civilisation.

The wastes created by Netherton Colliery were drained and landscaped in 1901 and then opened as a recreation ground. Gradually this was transformed into a park with bandstand and this fountain, which was moved from the junction of Halesowen Road and Cradley Road (see p. 18). It has disappeared in recent years without explanation. However, there is now some interest in regenerating Netherton's park. *(Reeves postcard: Trudi Blair)*

The Savoy cinema in Northfield Road was opened on 26 August 1936 and was a joint venture between Cecil Couper of Brierley Hill and Howard Bishop of Netherton, the latter becoming dissatisfied with his lease at the Public Hall. It survived with two three-day programmes a week until Christmas Eve 1960, and is seen here decorated for the 1953 coronation. The building was demolished in 2004. *(Gladys Bishop)*

Staff at Netherton's Savoy cinema, 1938. Charles Bishop, son of Howard Bishop, is in the centre, back row. Horace Fletcher, chief operator, is on the far right and his assistant is in the white coat. Nancy Baker is second from the right. *(NHG)*

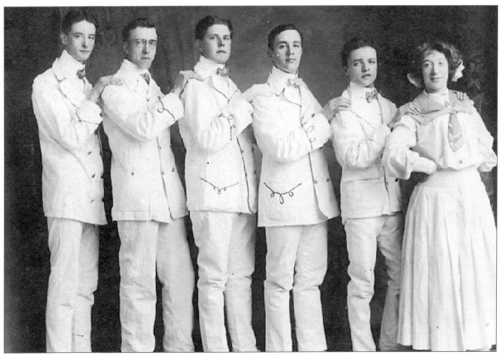

There has been plenty of dramatic and musical activity in Netherton, particularly associated with the churches and chapels. Here are the Blue & White Pierrots of 1906 with Arthur Jordan (famous tenor) third from left and Jack Doo fourth from left. *(Betty Doo Collection)*

Netherton Cricket Club, 1966. Messrs Shakespeare, Nash, Herbert, Passmore, Thompson, Armshaw, Rollason and Foley are standing. Seated, left: Fred Rollason (vice president and author of an excellent book about the NCC), J. Doughty, Sid Allport (captain and of Old Swan fame), C. Cotterill, and N. Wright (club chairman), plus tin pavilion. *(NHG)*

Netherton Football Club, *c.* 1960. On the right: Ron Corbett and Mr Willetts, joint managers. Jeff Willetts, captain, is in the centre. The team played on the Hingley's sports ground at Old Hill and folded when that ground was closed. *(Doris Corbett)*

Scouts in Netherton have been well organised, and in this 1938 picture we see them outside their old wooden headquarters near Bishton's Bridge. In recent years this has been replaced with a more modern building in Birch Terrace. *(Ernie Ward)*

1st Netherton Scouts Band assembles in Northfield Road in June 1953 before leading the Coronation Carnival Parade around town, and to the park. Messrs Hingley's had provided new instruments for the occasion. *(Ernie Ward)*

The Boys' Brigade has also been strong in Netherton and here they are in about 1980, passing Baker's Stores (their ice cream sign is seen top right!). Darren Mellor, son of the proprietors, is in the parade. *(Sheila Mellor)*

Netherton Toc H in 1934, in their old HQ in a cottage next to the Cricket Ground (Bagleys Lane). Branches of Toc H were established by ex-servicemen after the First World War, and met for fellowship and support of community activities, organising clubs for young people, camps and so on. The Netherton branch started in 1933 and 'received its lamp' on 11 December 1937. In 1943 the branch left this building and moved to 53 Griffin Street. *(Wesley Garratt)*

The St John Ambulance Brigade, Netherton Division, on their annual flag day, 15 August 1915. There is no shortage of Scouts and supporters. *(NHG)*

Coronation celebrations in Netherton Park, June 1953. Girls from the 1st Netherton Girls' Life Brigade (Ebenezer Baptist Chapel) are taking part in the Fancy Dress Competition. Left to right: Kathleen Jordan, Sheila Edwards, Maureen Davenport, Marian Griffin, Pat Baker. *(Harry Rose)*

Coronation celebrations in Netherton Park, June 1953. Netherton Coronation Carnival Queen, Jean Homer, sits next to the Mayor of Dudley, Alderman Silcox. Behind them is Chief Constable Johnson who is to judge the Fancy Dress competition. On the left are Jean's five attendants: Margaret Elwell, Jean Hipkiss, Rita Boulton, Joan Priest and June Robinson. Where are they now? *(Harry Rose)*

In the summer of 1977 the people of Netherton were celebrating the Jubilee – the 25th anniversary of the Queen's accession to the throne. Union Jacks are seen here in Arch Hill Street. The man in the white hat on the left is Harry Scriven, the well-known local butcher.

ACKNOWLEDGEMENTS

This book could not have been compiled without the considerable assistance of a vast number of people, with whom it has been wonderful to share an enthusiasm about Netherton. Very early in the project Sue Goodyear and Roy Hadley invited me to see the collection of Netherton material that had been assembled by the Netherton Local History Group – now subsumed by an Environmental Group, based in the Visitors' Centre at the Bumble Hole. Photographs from this collection have been credited to the group *(NHG)*. Everywhere else I went in Netherton, I received help and encouragement. The only unusual aspect of this project is that schools have been less eager to help than usual. Nevertheless, material is still pouring in as we go to press, and perhaps those who have not been able to contribute this time round may feel that a second volume will give them another chance! With great fear of leaving someone out, I would like to thank the following, arranged in alphabetical order:

Iris Alliband, Terry Alliband, Margaret Attwood, the Revd Billy Barnes, Jim Bate, Gladys Bishop, W. Boyd, Jack Brookes, Linda Button, the late Bob Carpenter, Olwen Chilton, Madge and Ray Cole, Doris Corbett, Rita Darby, Betty Doo, Winnie and Fred Emery, Garry Flavell, Wesley Garratt, Peter Glews, Sharon Green, Brian Grundy, Joe Guest, Ann and Peter Harris, Stan Hill, Keith Hodgkins, Joyce Holden, Alison Hurley (for Jeff Parkes), Stan Hutt, Ray Jones, Don Kirkby, Erena Little, Trevor Lowe, Ivor Lucas, Shirley Lynall, Sheila and John Mellor, Roger Mills, Betty Nash, the Revd Judith Oliver, Brian Payton, Christine Perks, Ken Pritchard, Ruth and Audrey Pugh, Brian Roberts, Geoff Roberts, Ernest Robinson, Dorothy Rollason, P.J. Shoesmith, John Tennent, Ron Thomas, Ernie Ward, Carole Welding (who provided the Harry Rose pictures), F.A. Wheeler, Joan White, Dave Whyley. Also to folks associated with Netherton's chapels who contributed to a book on that subject, and which has added to this project: these are Albert Willetts, Muriel Woodhouse, Cyril Wright and the Bert Beard Collection. Finally the staff at Dudley Archives who provided help and access to their photographic collection, which includes many photographs by Nethertonian Bill Massey.

To Ken Rock, for providing access to his postcard collection. To Movie Magic (Coseley) for photo processing. To Graham Beckley, Roger Crombleholme and Juliet Thompson for further work on photographs. To Terri Baker-Mills for coordinating my 'work–life balance' throughout the project.